My Dearest

FROM ISLAANTILLA !

THE
SOOD FAMILY
COOKBOOK

To see how it's done visit:
http://www.pinterest.com/hcindia/the-sood-family-cookbook/

THE
SOOD FAMILY
COOKBOOK

101 recipes for every home

APARNA JAIN

Collins

First published in India in 2013 by Collins
An imprint of HarperCollins *Publishers* India

Copyright © Aparna Jain 2013

ISBN: 978-93-5136-168-8

2 4 6 8 10 9 7 5 3 1

HarperCollins *Publishers*
A-53, Sector 57, Noida, Uttar Pradesh 201301, India
77-85 Fulham Palace Road, London W6 8JB, United Kingdom
Hazelton Lanes, 55 Avenue Road, Suite 2900, Toronto, Ontario M5R 3L2
and 1995 Markham Road, Scarborough, Ontario M1B 5M8, Canada
25 Ryde Road, Pymble, Sydney, NSW 2073, Australia
31 View Road, Glenfield, Auckland 10, New Zealand
10 East 53rd Street, New York NY 10022, USA

Book designed by Bonita Vaz-Shimray

Printed and bound at
Thomson Press (India) Ltd.

For Peggy maami and Raja maamu,
without whom neither I
nor this book would be;

And for my brother Arjun,
for whom this was originally written

The Sood Family tree depicted in Madhubani style

CONTENTS

From Near and Far

Light and Healthy

When under the Weather

Anytime Eats

Chutneys with Oomph

Sood Grog

Sweet Somethings

How to navigate this book

For easy reference, all recipes are titled in different colours

`Green` for **vegetarian** recipes
`Yellow` for recipes that contain **egg**
`Red` for **non-vegetarian** recipes

Conversion

I have been intuitive when it comes to using measures and weights. I was handed an assortment of recipes from different members of the family and each followed a different routine in the kitchen. I just went with the most instinctive for each recipe.

Most people have measuring cups and spoons in their kitchens, so some recipes follow that. For others which needed exact weight, for a few baking recipes for example, I have used g/kg, and for ingredients like daal, yogurt, veggies which one can pick up from the market according to weight, again I have used g/kg.

However, if you do believe in weights and measures, here is a quick guide:

1 tsp	5 ml
1 tbsp	15 ml
¼ cup	60 ml
⅓ cup	80 ml
½ cup	120 ml
⅔ cup	160 ml
¾ cup	180 ml
1 cup	240 ml

As far as baking is concerned, while temperatures are standard, I have noticed that depending on the brand and age of the oven being used, cooking time is often faster or slower than the time indicated. Please do keep checking your oven 5 minutes before indicated cooking time to check doneness. If your oven has a fan, chances are your dish will be cooked a little ahead of time.

A square tin holds approximately 25 per cent more than a round tin of the same size. If you use a square tin for a round tin recipe, keep the temperature the same, and turn the cake during baking. Remember that the corners tend to cook faster than the middle.

Oven Temperatures:

Fahrenheit (°F)	Celsius (°C)
225° F	110° C
250° F	130° C
275° F	140° C
300° F	150° C
325° F	165° C
350° F	177° C
375° F	190° C

Preface

'One day, you will have no choice but to get into a kitchen and cook.' Like many of my generation, I heard these words practically every week from my mother as she never tired of emphasizing the need for a woman to learn to cook. At the age of twelve and in my loudest phase of anti-gender stereotyping (at least when it came to chores I was told 'women should do'), I would tell her emphatically, 'I will never enter a kitchen. And I will get married to someone who can cook. So there!' And I would walk off in a teenage huff.

Needless to say, her prophecy came true! On my own, first abroad and then shuttling between cities across India, I began to learn how to cook. (My stint in hotel management didn't teach me kitchen skills, only managerial ones.) But even then I resisted the roti-daal-sabzi routine (I still don't know how to make a roti) and, instead, began to experiment with non-Indian cuisine. And that started me off on this foodie trip...

Over the years I honed my cooking skills. I also bought lots of recipe books although I use them less for cooking and more to look at the pretty pictures! Indian Accent, the restaurant in Delhi, helped me get over my naïve disdain for the mostly inartistic yet incredibly delicious Indian food. I was inspired. And I kept experimenting.

But it was a trip to my brother Arjun in Geneva that really kicked off the idea for this cookbook. In true Indian style, Behenji maasi sent her famous Himachali mutton and Peggy maami her equally celebrated chocolate cake. These were packed in the deep recesses of my bags, between my shoes and sweaters, and smuggled across to Geneva.

The cake was devoured within a few hours of my arrival. On a sugar rush, my brother invited fifteen friends over for dinner the next day and insisted we get them to try 'real Indian food'! Being the older bossy sister, who had already rearranged the furniture in his apartment at 06:00 hours while he was asleep, I decided to humour him and go the whole nine yards! (Seeing what a skinny mess my brother had become, surviving on Coca-Cola, ciggies, chips and stress, my maternal instincts had kicked in.)

We sat down to plan the menu. His idea of a 'simple Indian meal' went something like this: 'Behenji maasi's meat – the spicy one; madra like the one in Renu maasi's house with chana; sookhi daal like we used to have at home as kids...' I panicked and called all my aunts and uncles for the recipes, and was met with the same answer from all of them: 'Recipe? Bete, we don't write recipes, we just know what to do. And we really can't tell you how many teaspoons etc, it's all instinct.' So I scribbled down whatever little they were able to tell me.

Even as I got ready to cook, I realized that Arjun had all the kitchen appliances and gadgets, but no ingredients! So off I went to the nearest supermarket, to come back laden with fresh fruit, veggies and grain, including our famous 'Busmaati' as the Swiss call it.

I started my chopping and cooking, unable to understand half the instructions my family had given me over the phone. What does 'teen seeti' on the pressure cooker mean? Or 'masala tel chhod dega' or 'andaaz se'? But I knew that most of his friends wouldn't have eaten pahaadi food before, and so I could wing it a little. And that's just what I did!

A pleasant evening ensued and Arjun was so thrilled with the food and the success of his soiree that he cleaned up after dinner while I nursed a bottle of champagne to get over the five hours of cooking.

The next day, as we were reminiscing on the night before, I realized that many of us from the family were probably facing the same difficulties as we had the previous night. Living in nuclear families in cities around the world, we all wanted to find ways of replicating the specialties that certain family members were renowned for, but just didn't know how. It was also a way of reliving the memories associated with the foods.

And from that came the thought of documenting all the family recipes. I sat with the older generation (consisting of some pretty formidable elderly aunts, who had all their recipes in their heads) and tried to structure and document their instinctive approach to cooking. I worked with cousins who got their mise en place done by the cook but over time developed their own incredible fusion recipes. I began to collect recipes from Himachal Pradesh (since we are from Kangra and we eat pahaadi khaana at home), Sindh, Mangalore, Punjab, Tamil Nadu, Kashmir, Bengal, New York, Geneva and Thailand. This was collated into a private family cookbook that we distributed to the family and close friends over Christmas of 2005, courtesy Raja maamu.

Later, when I thought of updating the book, HarperCollins suggested that I publish it for a larger audience.

This cookbook is a gift from my family to you – when you move away from home and start a new job, when you go to study and are living in an apartment where some of you cook together at university, when you get married and set up your own home, when you crave something comforting, when you want to experiment with new recipes, when you need to know what to cook when sick, when you want food with flair or just want to try some home cooking from Himachal Pradesh. It doesn't follow the 'norms' of a cookbook in terms of standardization of measurements and number of people it serves (too puritanical); so just enjoy it as it goes.

Guten Appetit!

All-Day Breakfast

Breakfast was never an enjoyable part of my childhood. I remember Arjun and I waking up for school and being made to have egg and milk before we made our way to the bus stop. It was always a tedious affair, and whenever my mother's stern eyes weren't watching, I would hide the egg under a napkin or in my school bag and discard it en route to school. Over the years I have realized the importance of breakfast and though there are times I still play truant, they are few and far between.

Eggs
Ben-Adit

Ingredients

4 English muffin buns
4 thin ham slices

For the hollandaise:
3 large egg yolks
1 tbsp water
¼ tsp salt
¼ tsp + ¼ tsp red chilli powder (or any Mexican chilli you prefer)
1 tsp + 1 tsp + 1 tsp + 1 tbsp lime juice
250 g cold white butter, cut into 20 g pieces
2 tbsp chives, chopped

For the eggs:
8 large eggs
4¼ cups water
¼ cup white vinegar
1 tsp salt

Method

Making the hollandaise sauce:

Put a large pot of water on boil.

In a glass bowl (which fits comfortably over the pot of water without touching the water, like a double boiler) whisk the egg yolks, water, salt and chilli powder together for a minute or so.

When well mixed, place the glass bowl over the boiling pot of water, and bring the water to a low simmer, taking care not to let it touch the bowl.

Whisk vigorously over low heat and take the

There was a time when my cousin Aditya had the most demanding taste buds. A simple question like 'What would you like for breakfast?' would elicit an answer that went something like this: 'I want freshly poached brown eggs on a bed of spinach, placed gently on a multigrain bun, topped with hollandaise sauce and chives. On the side I would like breakfast sausage, fried in Tobasco, and some rösti. Also a grilled tomato, topped with herbs.' At which his mother would say to the cook, 'Baba ke liye fried anda aur toast.' And that was that. However, we all really enjoy Eggs Benedict and whenever I am so inclined, I whip up a decent hollandaise. Here is my quirky version of the Benedict called Ben-Adit.

glass bowl off the pot every 30 seconds to cool and avoid the yolk from cooking.

Each time, add a piece of cold butter and keep whisking, while putting back on the pot. Do this approximately 10 times. Your sauce should stay creamy and the eggs should not start scrambling.

At this point, about half the butter will have been used. When you take the bowl off the pot, add 1 tbsp lime juice and keep whisking.

When the last piece of butter has been added, add 1 more tbsp lime juice, sugar and red chilli powder.

Whisk for a few more minutes, till everything is nicely emulsified.

Taste to check if you need more lime. At this

point, add the chopped chives or whichever herb you can find easily.

Keep in a warm place. Reheat over the water once the poached eggs are ready.

Frying the ham:

In a small frying pan, lightly fry the ham and keep aside.

Drain on a kitchen towel.

Poaching the eggs:

In a large pot bring 4¼ cups of water to boil.

Add vinegar and salt.

As soon as the water boils, break the eggs one at a time into small cups.

Bring the water to a simmer and, using the back of a wooden ladle with a quick motion, stir the water to create a whirlpool effect.

Stop stirring and gently add an egg from its cup into the centre of this whirlpool. The white will cling to the middle of the egg and you will get an almost perfect poached egg shape.

Cook for about 5 minutes.

Repeat with all the eggs.

The secret to this recipe is to use enough water while poaching the eggs.

Assembling the Ben-Adit:

Cut each muffin horizontally into half and keep with both cut sides facing up.

Add a dollop of hollandaise on the open faces of the muffins.

Place a slice of ham on top of a muffin half.

Set the poached egg on top of the ham.

Drizzle some hollandaise sauce over the egg.

Repeat for each muffin half.

Garnish with herbs.

Serve immediately.

You can serve this with a grilled tomato. Sometimes I steam some spinach and use that as a bed before I add the egg on the muffin to get what is called an Egg Florentine. Play with flavours you prefer, both in terms of herbs and chillies.

Crispy Quinoa Roundels

Easy peasy

serves 4

I discovered quinoa sometime last year, and have been very happy with it. Not only is it a really healthy seed, but it also tastes great and can be used in a variety of ways, including as quinoa upma. We make this patty and love it for its crispiness, health and flavour.

Ingredients

1 cup quinoa
2 cups stock (see page 80)
1 tsp salt
3 tbsp olive oil

For the roundel:

½ cup cottage cheese (paneer), grated (optional)
1 carrot, grated
½ cup zucchini, grated and squeezed dry
1 spring onion or leek, chopped
½ tsp salt
½ tsp cumin powder (jeera)
½ tsp garam masala
3 eggs, whisked

For the yogurt topping:

8 tbsp hung yogurt
1 tsp garam masala
2 tsp cumin powder (jeera)

Method

Make the yogurt topping first:

Roast cumin powder on a pan for 30 seconds.

Whisk yogurt with garam masala. Keep yogurt in the fridge and roasted cumin separately on the counter.

Now make the quinoa:

Rinse the quinoa seeds several times under running water. This is to remove the outer covering called saponin which can give it a soapy, bitter flavour.

In a pot, boil the stock mixed with salt and then add the drained quinoa. Turn the heat down to the lowest temperature.

Cook for about 18-20 minutes till the water is absorbed and the quinoa seeds are cooked. At this point, the quinoa will look like little pearls and will have little spirals from each seed sticking out.

Remove from heat.

Fluff the quinoa up with a fork. and let it stand for 5 minutes.

Keep aside.

4

Next make the roundels:

In a large bowl mix together all the roundel ingredients.

Add the cooked quinoa to this and gently shape into little burger patties (should make 8 pieces) about 2 cm thick.

Use a large flattish pan to heat oil.

Gently slide the roundels into the pan and cook for about 4 minutes on each side on a gentle flame.

When one side gets crispy, flip it and fry the other.

When done, assemble two to a plate, either next to each other or on top of one another.

Now remove the yogurt dressing from the fridge and add a dollop of it on top of the roundel.

Garnish with roasted cumin powder.

You can add chilli powder to the roundel or the yogurt. I garnish the yogurt with a handful of chopped chives.

Quick Muffin Pan Eggs

The muffin pan is the best piece of equipment to have when making breakfast or brunch, especially for a crowd. I have used it to effectively make different breakfasts (mostly egg based) for 6-12 people. You can pretty much throw an assortment of items in the muffin pan and bake for a few minutes and voila – a perfectly healthy, easy-to-make breakfast.

Here are 4 things you can do with muffin pans or moulds which are simple to make, yet very fancy when popped out of the oven. Kids love these little breakfast muffins.

This is not a standardized recipe with a list of required ingredients and methods. This is where you use 'kitchen instinct'.

Muffin Pan Frittatas

This is great for kids who need a healthy egg breakfast.

Beat 3 eggs, add 2 egg whites and ¼ cup milk. Add a pinch of salt and pepper, 2 tbsp each of chopped onions, chopped red peppers, grated cheese, chopped ham and a tsp of chopped fresh chives. Mix into the muffin pans till each mould is ¾ full. Bake for about 15 to 20 minutes at 180°C till the eggs have risen like a mini soufflé.

Croque Fancy Aunty

This is perfect for a brunch, especially for ladies who lunch.

With a dough roller, roll out 6 slices of bread flat. Line the muffin pans with some melted butter and press the bread into the cups. Some of the bread will stick out, above the mould, which is fine. Add a slice of thin ham or chopped ham, a slice of tomato, a freshly cracked egg, and top with cheese if you like, or just herbs. Bake for 15 minutes at 180°C until the bread is toasty and the eggs baked beautifully.

Smoked Salmon Muffs

I like this for a large brunch because the pinkish smoked salmon makes for a beautiful shell.

Line the muffin pans with some butter. Add the smoked salmon slices to form a base within and around the sides of the muffin moulds. Add an egg, a pinch of salt and pepper and bake for 15 minutes at 180°C. Remove from the pan and top with some crème fraîche and chopped chives.

Crispy Potato Nests

I love these because of the crunch. If you do not eat eggs, you can use a bunch of vegetables in it.

Parboil 3 potatoes and cut them into matchsticks. Line the muffin pans with butter and add the matchsticks to completely cover the base and sides, creating a little nest of sticks. Add 1 tsp chopped onion, some bacon or ham bits, one egg for each muffin mould and a pinch of salt and pepper. Bake at 180°C for 15 to 18 minutes till the potatoes are baked and crispy. Serve hot.

Sindhi Sael Dabroti

Easy peasy

serves 8-10

Ingredients

For the chutney:

1 cup coriander leaves
1 lime, juiced
4 cloves garlic
1 onion, small
2 green chillies
½ tsp salt

For the curry:
2 tbsp vegetable oil
10-12 slices bread, slightly stale (it needs to be a day old to give body and absorb; fresh bread will crumble)
2 onions, chopped
3 cloves garlic
2 tomatoes, pureed
½ cup fenugreek leaves (fresh methi) or 2 tbsp dried fenugreek (sookhi methi)
2 tbsp tamarind paste
1½ cups water
½ tsp salt
½ tsp garam masala
100 g sev (fried gram flour bits)

This is a breakfast or brunch dish from Raajika maami's Sindhi family. She says it was so special that her mom reserved it for Sundays, when everyone had enough time to enjoy the dish. We often make it at home and it's almost like a thick Indian gazpacho with chutney. This serves many in the spirit of a true Sunday gathering. Halve the portions for a smaller group of people.

Method

In a mixer blend all the chutney ingredients and keep aside.

Heat oil in a pan and when hot, fry onions, garlic and turmeric.

Now add the chutney mix and fry for 2-3 minutes.

Add tomato puree, fenugreek leaves and garam masala and fry for 3 minutes.

Now add tamarind, salt and water and mix.

When the mixture boils, turn the flame off.

Add bread pieces and let them get coated generously.

Using a hand masher, mildly mash bread into this mix.

Garnish with crispy sev and serve hot.

Super Soft Idlis

Ingredients

3 cups rice (broken short-grained rice is best)
1 cup dhuli urad daal
1 tsp fenugreek (methi) seeds
1 tsp salt
1 tbsp ghee

My cousin Pinky makes the most amazing soft idlis all the time. Her idlis are the most coveted in the family. She serves them hot with chutney and sambar. Follow the instructions for her drumstick sambar (see page 46), substituting shallots or small onions for the drumsticks.

Method

Wash and soak daal and fenugreek seeds for at least 10 hours.

Grind the rice mixture with ½ cup water or so, in a traditional stone grinder. You get the electric-enabled stone grinders these days (these produce the softest idlis). If you don't have one, use a mixer.

When ground fine, remove to a large pot.

Now grind the daal and fenugreek seed mixture till fluffy. Add a little water if needed.

Remove and add to the bowl where you have stored the ground rice.

Add salt.

Mix gently with a ladle. The mixture should be thick and pasty, not watery.

Cover the mixture and leave to ferment overnight. The mixture will double in size.

The next morning, prepare your idli stands and steamer by greasing lightly with ghee.

Now carefully scoop out the mix and pour into the idli moulds.

Follow the instructions on your idli steamer for timing and amount of water.

Check if done by using a sharp knife to scoop the bottom of an idli out. If it comes out easily, without sticking, it is ready.

Place the idlis into a heat-retentive dish and serve along with sambar and chutney.

If you have leftover idlis, simply cut each into 4 pieces and add a tarka of ghee or oil with mustard seeds and curry leaves and serve as an evening snack with tea.

Home Food, Comfort Food

Our family is spread all over the country, but we Soods are originally Himachalis from a little village in Kangra called Deragopipur. I have to admit most of us haven't even been there, and the furthest most have gone is Shimla. My grandparents moved to Delhi several decades ago. My maternal grandfather and grandmother had ten children. TEN! My mother recounts this story of how every sister shared the task of making and serving the milk that all siblings had every night. Each child used to drink his or her milk differently: with 1 tsp sugar, with Ovaltine, with 2 tsp sugar, plain, with 1½ tsp sugar, with Bournvita and so on. It used to drive the sisters batty and, just to rile them up more, the brothers would keep changing their mind and concoctions.

My grandfather was a magnificent man, with incredible foresight and wisdom. My memories of him are steeped in just two magical words – churan and aampapad, which he used to keep locked away in his bedroom cupboard and give to us as treats when we visited. My grandmother was a petite yet formidable lady. (Bringing up ten kids is no easy task.) She had these lovely narangi trees in the house, and as kids of five and six, my cousin Aditya and I used to raid them, sneak off into a corner and eat the narangis (both of us love khatta). My grandmother used to get home in the evening, look at the trees, yell for our mothers (her daughter, my mother, and Aditya's mum, Peggy) and take off in her Pahaadi-Punjabi on how badly behaved we were. We learnt much later that, knowing us, she would count the precious narangis on her tree before leaving.

My grandfather had a very simple theory for his children. Marry whom you want (about 90 per cent of the marriages in the family are love marriages) and when you do, move out and set up your own home. (I mentioned he had great insight and vision.) So, luckily, my maasis and maamus got married to incredible people from different parts of the country, and the globe. We have Punjabi, Sindhi, American and Bengali aunts and uncles and obviously they all brought their unique food repertoire with them. This trend continued to the next generation and we added Kashmiri, Malayali, Mangalorean, Assamese, more American etc. Slowly and steadily each house acquired its own specialty aside from pahaadi khaana, which was the original staple diet at Connaught Place. This section is devoted to documenting our special pahaadi food and also the fantastic specialties that we now call our own from around the country.

Pahaadi Madra

Easy peasy · serves 4

My eldest maamu, Bhishamber or Birajee, was the managing partner at the famous Khyber restaurant in Bombay from the 1960s to the early 1990s. As young kids, we never realized what an institution Khyber was and we used to take the delicious butter chicken and other tandoori specialties for granted. All we knew was that when we wanted to have good old pahaadi khaana, there was no better place than his house. His wife (called badi bhabhiji by everyone else and maamiji by us) had spent a number of years in Shimla and had a delicate hand with food. Although we have some of her recipes, we still miss that magic touch, which made everything she cooked a treat.

Madra is one of the staple recipes from Himachal. In every household, you will find a different version of it. For instance, most people whisk the yogurt, but we don't. This is maamiji's version, which we follow in most of our homes. It is traditionally cooked in a heavy-bottomed Himachali pot called a bhaddu, but an open pressure cooker will do as well since it has a heavy bottom.

Ingredients

250 g chickpeas (kabuli chana) soaked
overnight without salt
500 g yogurt, thick and not beaten
3 cups water
½ tbsp pure ghee
½ tsp turmeric powder (haldi)
½ tsp cumin seeds (jeera)
1 tsp coriander powder (dhaniya)
salt to taste

For the tempering/tadka:
1 tbsp pure ghee
3 stalks green coriander, chopped
⅛ tsp red chilli powder

Method

For the madra:

In a pressure cooker, cook the chickpeas
with water on a high flame for about 15-20
minutes or till the chickpeas are tender.

In a separate pan, on a low flame, heat ghee.

Add turmeric powder, cumin seeds and
coriander powder.

Cook the spices on low heat for 20 seconds,
stirring constantly.

Add the chickpeas along with a couple of
teaspoons of water to this and cook till it
dries up (this takes about 5 minutes).

Add salt to taste.

The next step needs careful attention.

Using a largish ladle, gently spoon out a
dollop of yogurt without breaking it, and
place it gently over the chickpeas. Repeat
this two times till all the yogurt is used.

Do not stir

Cook on medium heat for 15 minutes.

The yogurt will become thicker and start
to solidify. That's when you know the dish
is done.

Keep aside.

For the tempering/tadka:

Heat ghee in a katori.

Add chilli powder. The ghee will look red.
Cook on a low flame for 20 seconds.

Add to the madra just before serving.

Add fresh coriander leaves.

Serve hot with boiled rice.

*You can also use peas and mushroom,
kidney beans or even leftover dry mutton
instead of the chickpeas to vary this dish.*

Pahaadi Palda

Super easy

serves 6

Palda is another staple of pahaadi khaana. Like madra, it is made with yogurt as a base. This is also my eldest maamiji's recipe and great to have with rice. It is light and easy on the stomach. The best part is that it is perfectly easy to whip up.

I am told that her grandson, Aatish, fed all of her recipes in his computer, while his ninety-year-old daadi dictated. Aren't family projects delightful?

Ingredients

450 g potatoes, peeled
500 g yogurt
2 tbsp ghee
1 tsp turmeric powder (haldi)
2 tsp cumin seeds (jeera)
2 tsp coriander powder (dhaniya)
½ tsp red chilli powder
salt to taste
2-3 cups water (for the potatoes)

Method

Peel the potatoes and cut into 1" square pieces.

Heat ghee. Add cumin, coriander powder, red chilli powder, turmeric and salt. Take care not to burn. Add the potatoes.

Add 2-3 cups water and continue to cook until the potatoes are done and the water evaporates.

Beat the yogurt with a 'madhani', an old-fashioned wooden beater (you can also use a stainless steel beater). Add enough water to get it all to one consistency. Keep it a little thick. Add a spoon of salt to this (only enough for the yogurt as the potatoes already have salt).

Just when you are ready to serve, heat the potatoes. Pour the yogurt mixture over it and stir very slowly on a low flame.

It should be heated only till one finger can be comfortably dipped in, or else the yogurt may curdle into paneer. Do not boil.

Serve hot. This dish does not take to reheating so it must be assembled just before serving.

> A few of us prefer a simpler palda cooked in mustard oil. You follow the same procedure as above, but use mustard oil instead of ghee.

Pahaadi Kaala Chana Khatta

This is another pahaadi dish that is a staple at a family lunch. I love it because I relish kaala chana. Also, it has a hint of khatta in it – a flavour I am partial to. Renu maasi says she makes her version with potatoes instead of black chana.

Ingredients

1 cup black gram with shell, soaked overnight (kaala chana)
3 tbsp mustard oil (sarson ka tel)
1 tsp white cumin (safed zeera)
¼ tsp ground fenugreek seeds (methi)
salt to taste
¼ tsp chilli powder
2 tbsp dried mango powder (amchur)
2 tsp coriander powder (dhaniya)
1 tsp fennel seeds (saunf)
2 tbsp chickpea flour (besan)
⅛ tsp asafoetida (hing)
3½ cups water
(optional)
2 tbsp coriander
leaves, chopped
½ tsp jaggery

Method

Boil the soaked black gram in a pressure cooker till it is tender.

Heat mustard oil in a wok.

When the oil is hot, add black gram and salt to taste.

Add cumin, fenugreek, chilli powder, dried mango powder, coriander powder, fennel seeds and chickpea flour to the wok.

Fry till you can smell the toasty chickpea flour.

Add the asafoetida.

Add water and cook till the curry is slightly thick (like besan kadhi).

Garnish with coriander leaves.

If you feel it is too sour, add a little jaggery.

Pahaadi Raajroopiyama

Somewhat easy

serves 6-8

This is a dry teliyamma daal from Pahaad. Renu maasi learnt this in her 'gaon', that is, Shimla. Of all the people I took recipes from, Renu maasi was the funniest. She would tell me the process and while I wrote it down, the ingredients would seem completely out of proportion. So I would question her. She would then think back and say, 'Oh haan, yeh to bahut zyaada ho gaya.' Needless to say, I tested each of her recipes twice over before including it here.

Ingredients

500 g sabut urad daal
3 tbsp mustard oil
⅛ tsp asafoetida (hing)
1" ginger, grated
1 bay leaf (tejpatta)
½ tsp fenugreek seeds (methi)
5 whole peppercorns
2 large cardamoms, crushed
2 small cardamoms, crushed
1 tsp cumin seeds (jeera)
2 tsp coriander seeds, crushed (dhaniya)
2" cinnamon
1 tsp chilli powder
¼ tsp turmeric powder (haldi)
1 tsp garam masala
1½ cup yogurt, beaten
10 raisins
¼ of a dry coconut, grated
10 almonds, soaked, peeled and slivered
2 tsp salt

Method

Soak the urad daal in water for at least an hour.

In a pressure cooker, add the daal with twice the amount of water (approximately 2 cups).

Cook the daal on a medium-high flame under pressure for three whistles. This will take 10-15 minutes.

Let it sit when done and open when cool. Check to see that the daal has split.

In a small wok, heat oil.

When hot, turn the gas on low and quickly add asafoetida, ginger, bay leaf, fenugreek seeds, peppercorns, big and small cardamoms, coriander, cumin, cinnamon, turmeric, chilli powder, garam masala.

Add the yogurt and stir till well cooked.

Add raisins, coconut and almonds.

Add the daal to this and if there is any water, open the lid and cook till the daal is dry.

Check for salt.

Serve immediately.

Pahaadi Chaach Waale Alu

Super easy

serves 4-6

This is a recipe from Mona maamu's home. It is a very simple recipe and while it looks like palda, it tastes different. It's great for when you come home on a weekday and are not sure what to whip up. It tastes delicious when served with Nepali chutney (see page 113)

Ingredients

5 potatoes, medium-sized
3 tbsp mustard oil
3 cups chaach (you could buy the readymade one)
1 tsp cumin seeds (jeera)
½ tsp turmeric powder (haldi)
1 tsp salt
½ tsp red chilli powder
1 green chilli, chopped
1" ginger, chopped

Method

Cut each potato into 4 pieces.

In a frying pan, heat mustard oil and add cumin seeds, ginger, chilli, salt and turmeric along with the cut potatoes.

Fry till potatoes change colour (about 7 minutes).

Turn the heat down and add chaach to the pan, stirring continuously.

Mash one potato and blend with the gravy (this gives the gravy body).

Cook till potatoes are tender.

Serve hot.

17

Pahaadi Fiddlehead Ferns

serves 6

Of all the vegetables I have seen, lungdu or lingdi (as they call it in Kangra), or fiddlehead ferns are definitely the prettiest. These ferns grow all over the hills during the monsoon. Whenever one of our drivers goes to his village, he gets me a kilo or two of these. While some people call it the Indian asparagus, others think it's more like a thick bean and some say it's a bit like ladies' fingers. The fronds are full of Vitamin A and the vegetable is supposed to be a great antioxidant. It doesn't travel very well since the fronds are delicate, so when you get some, cook them immediately. This fern has a somewhat hairy stem, so hold the stem by one hand, wrap a cloth around it with the other and rub down to get the bristles off. I just parboil it. You also get a mean lungdu ka achar in Himachal, made in mustard oil.

Ingredients

3 cups fiddlehead ferns
3 tbsp mustard oil
½ tsp cumin seeds (jeera)
½ tsp coriander seeds, lightly crushed (dhaniya)
¼ tsp turmeric powder (haldi)
1 tsp coriander powder
1 tsp cumin powder
1 tsp garam masala
1 tsp dried mango powder (amchur)
2 dry red chillies
salt to taste

Method

Trim the fiddleheads. (I cut off most of the stalk and keep the fronds and just a bit of the stem, but that's a personal preference.)

Place the fiddleheads in a large bowl of water and clean thoroughly to loosen any dust or grime.

Boil water in a large pot. Add the fiddleheads and cook until just tender, about 2-3 minutes.

Transfer the fiddleheads to a bowl of iced water for 5 minutes. Drain and keep aside.

Heat oil in a wok over medium-high heat.

Add cumin, coriander seeds and dry red chillies and cook for a few seconds till you get the aroma of the spices. Be careful not to burn them.

Add the dry powders and cook for a minute or so.

Add fiddleheads and cook for 2-3 minutes till nicely sautéed and covered with the masalas.

Taste to check the salt and serve immediately.

Pahaadi Mittha

Easy peasy

serves 4

As a child, I used to see this syrupy dry-fruit dish on the table and wonder why it was part of the main course and not served separately as dessert. After the main course, people would take a tablespoon of rice and heap this mix onto it and eat it to end their pahaadi meal. The concept of a sweet syrup on rice weirds me out, but all the pahaadis I know enjoy it with gusto (as does my American aunt), so there must be something to it. This dessert served with the main course is typically made during a dhaam (wedding feast). Mittha is made differently in different homes. Renu maasi puts salt in hers and Mona maamu uses a greater quantity of dry fruit. Experiment and come up with your own favourite concoction. Highly recommended if you have a VERY sweet tooth. This is Renu's recipe.

Ingredients

1 potato, medium-sized, grated and washed in cold water
1 tbsp ghee
1½ cups assorted nuts and dried fruits (walnuts, cashew nuts, raisins, apricots, pista, dry coconut)
½ tsp turmeric powder (haldi)
4 cardamoms
2 cups sugar
½ tsp salt

Method

In a pan, add ghee.

Squeeze the water out of the grated potatoes and add potatoes to the pan.

Fry till potatoes are light brown (approximately 7-8 minutes).

Add the nuts and dry fruit, salt and turmeric.

Fry for 2 minutes.

Add sugar and cardamom.

Fry for 2 minutes.

Add 1 cup water.

Let it boil for 10 minutes.

When the consistency is no longer water-like but slightly thick (it should coat the back of a spoon), take off the fire and serve with plain boiled rice.

Badi Bhabhi's Dahi Bhalla

serves 6

When trying to shortlist the recipes to get from everyone, Raajika maami wistfully said to me, 'Bhabhiji's bhallas are the best. You must try and get that recipe.' I balked. I am always intimidated by bhallas. The thought of grinding, shaping, frying and assembling is scary, but I certainly love eating them. Many of us just buy readymade bhallas and add the dahi bit at home. For the adventurous among you who want to use bhalla making as cooking therapy – here you go.

Ingredients

250 g urad daal (soaked overnight with skin)
500 g yogurt
2 tbsp + ½ cup green coriander leaves, chopped
2-3 green chilies, chopped
6 tbsp oil
1 tsp + 1 tsp salt
½ tsp + 1 tsp chilli powder
½ cup tamarind chutney without the banana
(see page 115)
1 tsp rock salt
2 tsp cumin powder, roasted (jeera)
15 raisins (optional)

Method

Soak daal overnight and remove the skin under running water.

Remove all the water and crush the daal in a mortar using a pestle or a wet grinder. (That's the traditional way but I used a mixer and it came out fine. For the last mix, I poured the batter into a bowl and mixed it with my hand, using long wide strokes for 3 minutes. This aerated the batter a lot more and helped make the final bhalla softer.)

Mix 2 tbsp coriander leaves and green chillies with the daal mixture.

Using clean but slightly moist hands, take a little bit of the batter into your palm and shape into a 3" flattish-on-top disc.

If you like raisins, add one or two in each disc.

Heat the oil in a wok till it starts smoking.

Put a drop of the bhalla mixture into the oil. If it sizzles and turns golden to rise to the top, the oil is ready. (This will also prove that your batter has been aerated enough.) If the batter doesn't rise to the surface, beat it a bit more with your hand to aerate it. Now start frying your flattened disks or quinelles a few at a time. (Don't crowd your wok, else the bhallas will stick to each other – give them room to roam.)

When they turn golden and rise to the surface, drain on a paper towel. In between batches, pause to let the oil reheat.

Soak the bhallas in warm salt water for about 5 minutes.

Remove from the water and gently squeeze dry. (This part can be a little intimidating, but if you use a gentle hand, you should be able to remove the oil and water mix from the bhalla.)

Keep the bhallas in the fridge.

In a bowl, beat the yogurt and enough water with a 'madhani' or yogurt whisk to get it all to one consistency.

Add salt and chilli powder to the yogurt. Keep in the fridge.

Just before serving, arrange the bhallas in a dish and pour the cold yogurt over it.

Top with tamarind chutney and coriander leaves. Decorate with red chilli powder, rock salt powder and roasted jeera powder.

Serve cold.

Pahaadi Rali-Mili Daal

serves 6

According to Raja maamu, this recipe was probably devised by someone who used all the leftover daals at the end of the month, put them in a bhaddu, and cooked them together. Sounds feasible. And thus a magnificent mixture of daals came together called Rali-Mili Daal. This is a mixture of 5 different daals, which is made in pahaadi homes and served with a mango chutney called Maani.

Ingredients

¼ cup arhar daal
¼ cup chana daal
¼ cup malka daal
¼ cup urad chilka daal
¼ cup hari sabut moong daal
1 tbsp + 2 tbsp oil
6 cups water
⅛ tsp asafoetida (hing)
1 tsp cumin seeds (jeera)
1 onion, chopped
2" ginger, chopped
2 cloves garlic, chopped
1 tsp green chilli, chopped
½ tsp turmeric powder
1 tsp coriander powder (dhaniya)
1 tsp chilli powder
1 tsp garam masala
1 tomato, chopped
¼ cup coriander leaves, chopped

Method

In a pressure cooker, fry daal in 1 tbsp oil for a minute.

Add water and pressure cook on high heat for 3 whistles.

When cool, open pressure cooker and see if daal is cooked. If not, leave on a high flame for a few minutes.

In a large frying pan, heat 2 tbsp oil.

Add asafoetida and cumin seeds.

Add onion, ginger, garlic and green chilli and fry till the onion is translucent.

Add dry masalas and cook for 30 seconds.

Add tomato and fry for 3 minutes.

Take 2 tsp daal from the pressure cooker and add into this mix to blend nicely.

Pour the entire masala mix from the pan into the daal in the pressure cooker.

Heat and add coriander leaves.

Serve hot with Maani (see page 110).

Khatti Daal

Easy peasy

serves 6

Three months after Raja maamu got married to his American bride, she was asked by one of the sisters if she was missing non-vegetarian food. Peggy was surprised; she had not even realized that since there was a puja in the family, everyone had been vegetarian for three months. That's how delicious Sood food is. Even a simple daal like this is yummy!

Ingredients

1 cup malka daal, cleaned and washed
2½ cups water
1 tsp coriander powder (dhaniya)
¼ tsp red chilli powder
½ tsp turmeric powder (haldi)
2 tsp salt
1 tsp cumin powder (jeera)
1" ginger, chopped
⅛ tsp asafoetida (hing)
2 tbsp amchur or 3-4 bakhari (dried whole mango pieces)
2 tbsp mustard oil

Method

Heat the oil in a pressure cooker.

When the oil is hot, add cumin, hing and ginger.

Add the daal. Fry for 2 minutes.

Add chilli, turmeric, coriander powder, salt and water.

Close the pressure cooker and let the daal cook on medium heat for 3 whistles.

When cool, open the pressure cooker.

Mix amchur or soak bakhari in a quarter cup of daal mixture.

Add this to the daal in the pressure cooker.

Leaving the pressure cooker open, bring this daal and amchur/bakhari mix to a boil.

Remove and serve with coriander leaves as a garnish.

The Unbeatable Pahaadi Mutton

Easy but long   serves 4-6

Ingredients

1 kg mutton, preferably with bones
1 cup hung yogurt
2 tbsp garlic paste
1 tbsp ginger paste
2 dry red chillies, crushed
2 green chillies
4 tsp salt
½ cup + 3 tsp ghee
300 g onions chopped
3-4 large cardamoms
3-4 small cardamoms
2" cinnamon
6-7 cloves
1 bay leaf (tejpatta)
1 cup freshly made tomato puree
(I just blend 6 tomatoes without the
skin in a mixer)
3 tbsp coriander powder (dhaniya)
3 cups water
1 tsp garam masala
2 tbsp chopped coriander
4 tsp salt
2 pieces charcoal

This is the BIG ONE. Behenji maasi's mutton is legendary: we all call it Behenji ka mutton. While this is a feat of art and love (as my maasi never fails to remind us – it takes a long time to make), it is worth learning how to make it. Believe me when I say this will leave you licking your fingers and gnawing the bones. The bit that gives it the added punch is the coal dhunni at the end. Don't miss that step.

Method

Marinate the cleaned, washed mutton pieces for a minimum of 6 hours or overnight in the refrigerator with yogurt, garlic, ginger, red chillies and salt.

The next day, take the mixture out of the fridge and bring to room temperature.

Heat the ghee, using a pressure cooker or a pan which has a nice heavy bottom.

Add all the whole spices (cinnamon, cardamoms, cloves and bay leaf).

When the cardamoms swell up, add all the onions and cook until they are lightly browned. This can take a while, but don't hurry the process.

Add the mutton.

You will need to now stay near the pot and stir the mutton every couple of minutes. The mutton will be creamy colour (because of the marinade), but once heated, you will slowly see the water from the yogurt thinning. Keep the mutton cooking and keep it browning. Turn it often so that it does not stick to the bottom of the pan.

Continue to do this till the mutton has taken on a deep brown colour. This takes about 40 minutes of cooking and turning. Add a few drops of the leftover marinade yogurt water every time the mutton sticks to the bottom.

When your mixture is a deep dark brown, add the tomatoes and coriander powder.

Stir this mixture occasionally. When the mix is somewhat dry, add water.

At this point, I cheat and use the pressure cooker, but you can actually slave over the stove like Behenji maasi does for an hour or more (love, people, love!). I cook in the pressure cooker on a medium flame for three whistles.

After it cools, open the pressure cooker and sprinkle 1 tsp garam masala over the dish.

Add the chopped coriander.

Just before serving, put a piece of charcoal on the fire.

When it is well lit (this takes almost 10 minutes), put it into a little bowl and pour a little ghee over it.

Place this bowl on top of the mutton mix in the pot and cover it for two minutes till the smoke infuses the mutton.

When ready to serve, remove the charcoal bowl.

Put the mutton in a serving bowl and garnish with chopped coriander.

Pahaadi Dhaniya waala Chicken

Easy peasy

serves 6

This is my youngest uncle Kaka maamu's very own pahaadi concoction. He insists that this will be the 'star' of the book. When I spoke with his wife Raajika about this dish (I was sceptical as Kaka maamu wasn't quite forthcoming about all the seemingly missing ingredients), she said that the reason they loved this chicken was that it did not come from the 'usual suspect' bhuna masala base that is typical of most north Indian food. It is an easy, light, low-on-spice dish. This is best cooked in a handi and MUST be served immediately. It's very easy to make and must be tried at least for the 'enthusiasm' with which it was given for this book. It tastes of coriander, coriander and coriander.

Ingredients

50 g butter
1 cleaned chicken, cut into 16 pieces
1 tsp coriander seeds, pounded
1 glass milk (room temperature)
50 g coriander stems, chopped
50 g coriander leaves, chopped
100 g cream
3 green chillies, chopped, deseeded

Method

Melt butter in a pan.

Put in the chicken pieces and sauté till the pieces turn white.

Add the cracked coriander seeds and stir fry for two minutes.

Add milk and cook this mix for 3-4 minutes.

Add chopped coriander stems and leaves and cook for 4-6 minutes.

Keep stirring occasionally while the chicken is simmering on a low flame.

Add the cream. When the sauce is semi-dry – it should cling to the back of a spoon – and the chicken is tender, remove from the fire.

Serve immediately.

Sheikhland Chicken

serves 4

My earliest memory of my cousin Sonal in the kitchen is as recent as 2006 when I was in London. I went over to her house where she made a fantastic 2-minute improvised Khow Suey. Sonal says she never entered the kitchen while growing up (man, we sisters!) and she recently felt this need to create something involving both labour and love, and from there came this recipe. She made this first while living in Dubai, therefore the name.

Ingredients

3 chicken breasts, diced
2 tbsp olive oil
6 curry leaves
6 cloves garlic
1" ginger, chopped
2 large onions, chopped
3 large green chillies, sliced lengthwise
4 cardamoms
1 tsp coriander powder (dhaniya)
1 tsp cumin powder (jeera)
1 tsp salt
2 tomatoes, pureed in a mixer
3 tbsp yogurt
½ tsp turmeric powder (haldi)
½ cup water

Method

Heat oil in a pan.

Add curry leaves and cardamoms until you see the cardamom pods pop.

Add garlic and ginger. As soon as it browns, add onions and wait till they turn slightly brown.

Add chillies, coriander powder, cumin powder and salt and fry briefly.

Add diced chicken pieces and let them turn brown.

Add tomato puree little by little to let it amalgamate with the chicken.

Mix yogurt with turmeric and water and add this too.

Cover and let it cook until semi-dry and all the spices are well integrated in the dish.

Serve hot with chappatis or rice.

Bengali Mustard Fish

Ingredients

½ kg bhetki fish, cut into 3"x3" pieces
¼ tsp + ½ tsp turmeric powder
1 lime, juiced
2½ tsp mustard seeds (sarson)
1½ tsp poppy seeds (khus)
8 cloves garlic
4 green chillies, slit lengthwise into 4 pieces each
2 tbsp + 3 tbsp mustard oil
1 tsp red chilli powder
3 cups coconut milk
1 tsp fresh coriander, chopped
2" ginger, julienned
salt to taste

Rama maami's repertoire was largely seafood based. All the recipes she sent me had fish, prawns, even lobster. I suppose being in Burlingtons, opposite Mocambo on Park Street, with its famous baked crabs and other fabulous seafood, provided ample inspiration. I told her to pick one recipe from her seafood array, and she zeroed in on this one. The common thread in all her food: super simple and fabulous to taste.

Method

Marinate the fish in turmeric and lime juice for 30 minutes.

In a mixer, make a paste of mustard seeds, poppy seeds, garlic and green chillies.

Add 2 tbsp mustard oil to a pan. Wait till the oil turns a deep orange red and then add the turmeric and the paste.

Fry lightly till the oil separates from the paste.

Add red chilli powder, salt and green chilli.

Add coconut milk and cook on a low flame till curry thickens.

In a separate pan, cook bhetki in mustard oil on both sides for a few minutes till it is done.

To serve, remove the cooked fish into a serving plate and spoon the sauce over the fish.

Garnish with coriander and ginger.

Sindhi Fenugreek Bhetki

Raajika maami says that while growing up they used to eat very simple light Western food on weeknights. Weekends, however, were reserved for the big treats in the kitchen and her mother made a lot of traditional Sindhi food. Her mom used to plate up every dish beautifully and Raajika remembers that everyone used to get one full fish to themselves. Raajika says this is a 'really yummy, yummy, yummy dish'. It is usually served with khichdi.

Ingredients

½ kg fish fillet (preferably bhetki)
¾ cup fresh methi leaves (fenugreek)
salt to taste
6 tbsp vegetable oil
1 large onion, chopped
1 tsp coriander powder (dhaniya)
½ tsp turmeric
3 tbsp yogurt, beaten
5-6 cloves of garlic, chopped
1 tsp of ginger paste
100 g coriander leaves, chopped
3 tomatoes, medium-sized, chopped
½ cup water
3-4 green chillies slit lengthwise

Method

Rub some salt on the fish fillets and set aside.

Heat oil in a non-stick frying pan.

Add onion and sauté till translucent.

Mix coriander powder and turmeric in the yogurt and keep aside.

Add garlic, ginger, methi and coriander leaves and cook till the methi becomes glazed and the oil separates from the dish.

Add tomatoes and cook on low heat till they are tender.

Add water and cover and cook on medium heat till the water is almost absorbed.

Add fish fillets to the pan.

Lift the paste from the sides of the fillets and cover the fish (do not stir or the fillets will crumble).

Pour yogurt and coriander powder mixture over the fillets to cover them.

Cook for 5-7 minutes on medium heat. Add chillies.

If the fish looks too dry, heat a ladle of oil and pour on top to glaze it.

Serve immediately.

Aphrodisiacal Shrimp Biryani

This is actually a prawn biryani recipe that comes from Nita's Mangalorean family. When Nita made it for the first time for my cousin Aditya in Delhi, he was very sceptical because he could not imagine a biryani made with prawn. But after one mouthful, he quickly cleaned up his first helping and all that was left in the serving platter! Ever since, 'shrimp rice', as Aditya insists on calling it, is a regular on their menu. He says it evokes a feeling of complete bliss.

Ingredients

For the ghee rice:
1¼ cups Basmati rice
2 cloves
3 2" cinnamon
3 cardamoms
2 bay leaves (tejpatta)
2 sprig curry leaves
2 onions, medium-sized, sliced
1 tbsp ghee
½ tsp salt
water: 1.5 times the volume of rice

For the shrimp curry:
24 shrimps, medium-sized, deveined
3 tbsp oil
3 onions, medium-sized, chopped
1 tomato, medium-sized, chopped
1 tsp sugar
10 curry leaves
salt to taste

To be ground to a paste:
2 dry red chillies
6 green chillies
1" ginger
8 pieces garlic
4 cloves
2 2" cinnamon
2 cardamoms
a pinch nutmeg
1 tsp cumin seeds (jeera)
1 tbsp poppy seeds (khus)
12 cashew nuts
1 tbsp coconut, grated
1½ tsp tamarind paste
½ tsp turmeric powder (haldi)
2 cups fresh coriander
curry leaves, chopped

For the garnish:
2 onions, sliced

Method

For the ghee rice:

Heat ghee. Put in the cloves, cardamom, cinnamon and bay leaves.

Add onions and fry till translucent.

Add rice and fry a little.

Add the required salt and water and cook the rice until almost done. (This should take about 7-8 minutes, but may vary slightly depending on the type of rice. The rice should be just right or a little undercooked. When you do the layering in step 10, it will cook a little more.)

For the shrimp curry:

Heat oil in a pan and fry onions for about 12 minutes till light brown.

Add tomato and curry leaves and fry till soft and well mixed with onions. (This will take about 6 minutes.)

Add ground masala and fry well for about 10 minutes.

Add shrimps, sugar and salt to taste. Cook till done. (Time will vary depending on the size of the prawns and how long they take to cook.)

For the garnish, fry two onions till dark brown and keep aside. (This is optional. Nita only does it for special occasions.)

Layering:

In a handi, take a little ghee, spread a layer of rice, then a sprinkle of fried onions and then a layer of the prawn curry. (If no space for a handi in a city kitchen, use a non-stick wok that has a tight lid.)

Continue the rice-onion-prawn curry layering until you have used it all up.

With a spoon, make some holes in the layered rice and put a little oil or ghee.

Place the closed vessel on a tawa and let it cook on a very low flame for 20 minutes.

Mangalorean Fish Curry

serves 4

This is the only way I like eating a fish curry – sour and coconuty. My sister-in-law Nita says there are two ways of making this. One is to extract coconut milk and add it to the wok in stages. The other and easier way is to grind the coconut along with the masalas.

Ingredients

500 g fish (sole or sear)
Coconut milk, from one medium-sized coconut (you can substitute with 200ml packaged coconut milk)
1 onion, chopped
1" piece garlic, chopped
2 green chillies, chopped

Masala to be ground:
8 dry red chillies, roasted
1 tbsp coriander seeds (dhaniya)
¼ tsp mustard seeds
½ cumin seeds (jeera)
½ tsp fenugreek seeds (methi)
1 onion
10 garlic cloves
8 peppercorns
2 tsp tamarind paste
salt to taste

Method

Grind red chillies, coriander, mustard, cumin and fenugreek seeds with onion, garlic and peppercorns.

In a wok, put in ground masala, and the second and third coconut milk.

Boil well for 5 minutes.

Add the onion, garlic, chillies and boil for another 5 minutes.

Add the first coconut milk.

Check for salt and sourness. If need be, tamarind paste could be diluted with water and added at this stage.

Add cleaned fish. Do not let it boil too much at this stage as the fish cooks quickly.

Grind grated coconut with water three times to get three types of milk. The first will be the thickest liquid, the second will be thinner and the third the runniest and mildest tasting.

Not-so-spicy Andhra Meat

serves 4

When my cousin Priti went to Dubai to meet her eldest bhabhi, she was taught this meat preparation. This semi-dry Andhra Roast Mutton is not only simple to make but also delicious. It is best eaten with paranthas.

Ingredients

½ kg meat, diced
1 tsp red chilli powder
1 tsp salt
1" piece ginger
4 cloves garlic
1 onion finely chopped
6 onions, medium-sized, diced
4 green chillies, slit lengthwise
1 tbsp + 1 tbsp vegetable oil
12 curry leaves
1½ cups water
¼ cup coriander leaves to garnish

garam masala:
4 cloves
4" cinnamon
2 big cardamoms
2 small cardamoms

Method

Marinate meat for an hour with ginger, garlic, red chilli powder, salt and finely chopped onion for 4 hours or overnight in a non-metal container.

In a heavy-bottomed pan, put 1 tbsp cooking oil. Wait till the oil is hot.

Throw in the garam masala and fry for 2 minutes.

Add marinated meat and keep stirring till the meat releases a little water.

Add water.

Let the meat boil, and then cover with lid and simmer till it becomes semi-dry. (If the water dries up too quickly and meat is not tender, you may keep adding more water.)

In a small tempering pan, add 1 tbsp oil.

Throw in the curry leaves.

Add diced onions and fry till pinkish brown.

Add meat and keep frying till it turns a deep reddish brown.

Add fresh coriander and green chillies.

Serve hot.

Kundapur Ghee Roast

serves 6

Nita's sister stays in Kundapur, near Mangalore, which is famous for this ghee roast, which we absolutely love. We now make it regularly at home and serve it with appam or neer dosai when we have the patience to make these, else we eat it with parantha.

Ingredients

1 kg chicken, washed and cut into bite-sized pieces
½ cup yogurt
½ tsp turmeric powder (haldi)
½ tsp salt
1 tbsp lime juice
7-8 dry red Begdi chillies
3 dry red Kashmiri chillies, small
salt to taste
2 tsp jaggery
1 sprig curry leaves
1 tbsp + 2½ tbsp + 1½ tbsp ghee
8 black peppercorns
3 cloves
¼ fenugreek seeds
1½ tbsp coriander seeds
½ tsp cumin seeds
8 cloves garlic
1½ tbsp tamarind paste

Method

Marinate chicken in yogurt, turmeric powder, lime juice and salt for a minimum of 4 hours or overnight in the refrigerator.

Roast both types of red chillies on a low flame for 2 minutes and keep aside.

In the same pan, add 1 tsp ghee and roast fenugreek seeds, coriander seeds, cumin seeds, cloves and peppercorns for 3 minutes. Remove and cool.

Grind the roasted red chillies and spices with garlic and tamarind to a fine paste. This is your ground masala.

Heat 2½ tbsp ghee in a heavy-bottomed pan, place the marinated chicken along with the marinade and simmer for 20 minutes or till it is almost cooked.

Remove the chicken pieces and keep aside. Pour the remaining liquid from the pan into another bowl (refer to this as marinade).

In the same pan, sauté the ground masala in the rest of the ghee on a low flame for 8-10 minutes. The ghee will start to separate from the masala.

Add the chicken pieces and mix well. Add marinade kept aside and jaggery and cook on medium heat for 3-5 minutes. Add salt to taste and mix.

Reduce flame, cover and cook till the chicken is done. The chicken should be coated with a thick masala. Remove the lid and continue cooking till the masala is thick.

Serve with rice, appam, neer dosai or as a starter.

Mangalorean PORK Vindaloo

serves 4

Vindaloo is an Indian dish with meat, usually pork, wine and garlic. The name is derived from a Portuguese dish and is very popular along the Goan and Mangalorean coasts. This spicy dish is often served on festive occasions and has been a regular at every Christmas Eve dinner at Nita's parental home in Mangalore. The pork should be fresh so that it cooks in the time indicated.

Ingredients

½ kg pork, boneless
3 onions, large, chopped
3 tomatoes, medium-sized, chopped
1½ tbsp oil
salt to taste
2-3½ cups water
3 tbsp white wine vinegar; half the amount if you are serving the same day

Vinegar is a must. If you plan to use the curry the following day, the excess water, pungency and sourness will get absorbed and balanced. Nita always cooks it a day in advance.

To be ground to a masala:
5 long dry red chillies
5 small dry red chillies
1½ tsp cumin seeds (jeera)
½ tsp mustard seeds
15 cloves garlic
1 tsp pepper
1 onion
½ tsp turmeric powder (haldi)
3 cinnamon sticks
3 cloves

To be ground to a paste:
2 dry red chillies
6 green chillies
1" ginger
8 cloves garlic
4 cloves
2 sticks cinnamon
2 cardamoms
⅛ tsp nutmeg
1 tsp cumin seeds (jeera)
1 tbsp poppy seeds (khus)
12 cashew nuts
1 tbsp coconut, grated
1½ tsp tamarind paste
½ tsp turmeric powder (haldi)
2 cups coriander leaves, chopped

Method

Heat oil in a pan or pressure cooker (without the lid on). Add onions and fry till brown.

Add ground masala and fry well till the raw smell of the masala goes. This will take about 3-4 minutes.

Add tomatoes and fry till they let out oil or move towards the centre of the pan (that is, they stop sticking to the sides). This takes anywhere between 8 and 10 minutes.

Add pork, salt and boil. If you are boiling in a pan, you will need to add 3 cups water and cook for about 40-80 minutes, depending on how tender the meat is. If you are cooking the pork in a pressure cooker, set it on high heat for 5 minutes till it whistles once.

Continue to cook on medium heat for 10 more minutes. Open the pressure cooker after it has cooled to check if the pork is cooked and tender. If not, put the lid back on and cook for another 5 minutes.

When cooked, add the vinegar.

Serve with sanna, appam or steamed rice.

> *Sanna and appam are Goan and Mangalorean specialties, typically made from fresh toddy. Depending on your preference for thickness of gravy, you can reduce the tomatoes and increase the vinegar.*

Butter Chicken in a hurry

Easy peasy

serves 4

My cousin Tunni Bhai lives in Canada with his wife Annu and my twin nephews. We know that living without help is tough. Annu didi's weekends are spent in the kitchen and, while some cooks drink wine while cooking, her stimulant is tea, copious cups of tea. Her kitchen habits and recipes are geared for efficiency so that they don't require minute-to-minute attention. Her butter chicken is so popular that her sons used it to leverage their popularity with the girls at their school and with colleagues at workplaces. Every time there is a potluck, the demand is for the butter chicken. This is not your overly liquidy butter chicken; it is a nice, thick, almost bordering on butter chicken masala recipe. It tastes great with roti or naan. You can substitute the chicken with paneer.

Ingredients

1 kg chicken, cut into pieces
75 g butter
1 tsp dry fenugreek leaves (kasoori methi)
¼ cup fresh coriander leaves, chopped
6 tbsp tomato sauce (see page 105) without oregano in it
3 tsp almond/cashew powder
3 tbsp light cream
½ tsp garam masala

For the marinade:
1½ tsp ginger paste
2 tbsp garlic paste
4 tbsp tandoori masala (you can use any good masala available in your neighbourhood store)
½ tsp green chilli, chopped
3 tbsp yogurt
1 tsp cumin seeds
3 tbsp olive oil
2 limes, juiced
1½ tsp turmeric
½ tsp red chilli powder
1 tsp salt

Method

Mix all the marinade ingredients together and marinate the chicken between 30 minutes to 4 hours.

Heat a thick-bottomed pan.

Add butter. Then add the marinated chicken. It will look quite viscous because of the olive oil in it.

Cook on high heat until all the liquid of the yogurt dries up. This takes between 15 and 20 minutes.

At some point, the water will dry and the butter fat will come to the top. Add dry fenugreek leaves. Mix well.

Spread the tomato sauce all over the butter chicken. Mix and simmer till the tomato sauce blends in nicely. This should take about 5 minutes.

Add cashew or almond powder to thicken.

Add the light cream.

Add garam masala. Simmer till the almond makes the butter chicken thick and gives it body and texture.

Take off the gas. Garnish with coriander leaves and serve.

Andhra-style Chicken Biryani

Easy peasy

serves 6

Right from my India Today *days, one of my favourite haunts has been Andhra Bhawan. I absolutely love the food there, and I really enjoy their Sunday Biryani. In my quest to replicate a good Andhra biryani, I mishmashed two recipes and came up with this version which is a big hit. It is spicy and loaded with mint and coriander and is not your delicate Nizami Hyderabadi Biryani. I love eating it with a raita, fried papad and fried yogurt chillies. It involves a fairly long prep process so make sure you start it way in advance.*

Ingredients

1 kg chicken, with bones
1½ cups rice, soaked for 30 minutes in milk
2 tbsp + 1 tbsp ghee
4 eggs, hard boiled
3 onions, sliced

For the marinade:
2 tbsp ginger
½ cup coriander leaves, chopped
½ cup mint leaves, chopped
1 cup yogurt, hung
8 green chillies
2 onions, sliced and lightly fried
2 tsp salt
2 tsp garam masala powder

For Masala 1:
3" ginger, grated
4 cashew nuts, chopped fine
6 cardamoms
2 sticks of cinnamon
1 bay leaf (tejpatta)
2 star anise
2 tsp cumin seeds (jeera)
1 tsp red chilli powder

For Masala 2:
4 tomatoes, pureed
2 tsp salt
1 tsp coriander powder (dhaniya)

Method

In a mixer, add all the marinade ingredients and blend well.

Marinate the cleaned chicken pieces in this mix and cover and leave overnight in the fridge.

The next day, bring the chicken and marinade to room temperature.

In a heavy-bottomed pot (which has a tight-fitting lid) add 2 tbsp ghee.

Add Masala 1 and fry for 2-3 minutes, taking care not to let it burn.

Add chicken and fry well till the marinade starts to cook. After 5-6 minutes of stirring, when you see the chicken has taken on a greenish hue, add Masala 2.

Stir well till the tomato puree is well mixed and then cover the pot for 7 minutes till the chicken is almost cooked.

In a pressure cooker, add 2 tbsp ghee and then add the rice. Fry for 2-3 minutes.

Add chicken and all the chicken gravy. (This should be enough to cook the already soaked rice in. If you feel the chicken is dry for some reason, add 1 cup water.)

Stir and then cover and let it cook on a medium flame for 2 whistles (should take 11-12 minutes). If not using a pressure cooker, cover the pot with a tight lid and cook as you usually would.

In the interim, fry the sliced onions in a wok till crispy. Drain on a kitchen paper and keep aside.

Peel the eggs and cut into quarters.

When the biryani is ready, top with eggs and fried onions and serve.

Kashmiri Yakhni Mutton

serves 4-6

Another recipe from Sunandini, who learnt from a very old family cook of theirs, Nagerchand. This is a famous Kashmiri Pundit dish and is made with yogurt as a base. You can substitute the mutton with chicken but it isn't half as nice. Serve this dish with plain boiled rice.

Ingredients

1 kg mutton (preferably ribs or other fatty mutton) cut into medium-size chunks
1½ cups water
1½ tsp salt
4 cloves
2 bay leaves (tejpatta)
2 black cardamoms, crushed
4 green cardamoms, crushed
2 tsp ginger powder (called sund in Kashmir)
3 tsp fennel powder (saunf)
4 cups yogurt, whisked well
6 tbsp vegetable oil/ghee
1 tsp garam masala powder

Method

Boil the water in a pan.

Put in the mutton, salt, cloves, bay leaves, black cardamoms, green cardamoms, ginger and fennel powder.

Cover and cook till the mutton is tender (approximately 30 minutes).

Take 3 tbsp from the hot mutton gravy and add the whisked yogurt, in a separate bowl, to make it warm.

Pour the yogurt over the meat, stirring constantly till it boils.

Keep stirring till the gravy is smooth and thin, a custard-like consistency. It is important to keep stirring or the gravy will curdle.

After 15 minutes of simmering this mixture, make the tadka (tempering).

Heat ghee till it sizzles and pour over the mutton.

Sprinkle the garam masala over this and cover the dish.

After two minutes remove from heat.

Serve hot.

Kashmiri Kofta Curry

serves 4

My cousin Yudhishthira is a keen foodie. His wife Sunandini is popular for many things, particularly her lovely singing voice and her ability to churn out great food. Being Kashmiri, she has some incredible recipes, and this kofta recipe is one of her best.

Method

Take the minced meat in a bowl, add red chilli powder, ginger powder (¼ tsp), aniseed powder (1 tsp), asafoetida, yogurt (1 tbsp), oil (2 tbsp), cardamom, Bengal gram powder and 1 tsp salt.

Knead well with your hand till the spices are well blended and the mixture starts to grease your hands.

Make 15 equal portions of the mixture. On a flat greased surface, roll each portion gently into a 3"-long sausage or kofta. Keep aside.

Heat oil in a deep pan. Mix together red chilli powder and yogurt. Add to the oil, stirring briskly. When the oil separates, add water and stir again.

Add the remaining ginger powder, aniseed powder and garam masala powder, the remaining asafoetida, cloves, bay leaves, cardamom skins and remaining salt into the pan. Cook till the gravy comes to a boil.

Carefully slide in the koftas, one at a time, and cook on a high flame till the gravy starts to thicken. Lower the flame and cook, stirring gently till the oil separates.

Serve hot with rice.

Ingredients

500 g lamb mince (keema), without fat, finely ground
1½ tsp red chilli powder
¼ tsp + ¾ tsp ginger powder (saunth)
1 tsp + 2 tsp aniseed powder (saunf)
¼ tsp of asafoetida (hing)
1 tbsp + 2 tbsp yogurt
2 tbsp + 4 tbsp oil
3 big cardamoms, crushed, skins kept aside
2 tbsp whole Bengal gram, roasted, powdered
salt to taste
1 cup water
½ tsp garam masala
4 cloves
2 bay leaves (tejpatta)

Brinjal Pachadi

Easy peasy

serves 2-3

Ingredients

1 big round brinjal
1 kg yogurt (make sure it is not sour)
¾ cup coconut flesh
2 green chillies, chopped
1 tsp + 1 tsp mustard seeds
1 dry red chilli, broken into little pieces
5-6 curry leaves
2 tsp salt

This recipe too comes from Pinky. After her marriage, Pinky learnt a number of south Indian recipes and this is one she loved. She says it leaves her with a 'contented feeling'. This recipe is to be eaten with rice.

Method

Roast brinjal over a gas fire till it is tender from inside and you can peel the skin easily.

When cool, peel the skin and stem and mash the brinjal a bit.

In another bowl, whip the fresh yogurt with 1 tsp salt.

In a mixer, blend green chillies and 1 tsp mustard seeds with coconut. Use very little water so that it looks like a thick chutney. (It should not be watery.)

Add this mixture to the yogurt and mix well. Add salt.

Make sure the brinjal is hot and then add the yogurt mixture to it.

Heat 1 tsp oil and add mustard seeds, a red chilli and 5 curry leaves for a quick tadka (tempering). Pour on top of the brinjal-yogurt mixture.

Serve immediately.

Spicy Drumstick Sambar

Easy peasy

serves 6

Ingredients

Stage 1: Pre-cooking the drumsticks
3 long drumsticks (green and thick, not woody and dry)
⅛ tsp turmeric
⅛ tsp salt
water

Stage 2: Making the sambar
1 tbsp vegetable oil
1 large onion, chopped
1 large tomato, chopped
1¼ cups arhar daàl (soaked for an hour)
½ + ½ tsp turmeric powder (haldi)
½ + ½ tsp salt
½ tsp red chilli powder
2 cups water
2 tsp sambar powder
2 tsp tamarind paste
6 curry leaves

Stage 3: Tempering
½ tsp vegetable oil
1 tsp mustard seeds
2 dry red chillies

On visiting her mother-in-law in Chennai for the first time, Pinky saw a beautiful tree in the garden. She learnt that the long pods hanging from it were drumsticks. Her mother-in-law plucked a few and proceeded to teach her this spicy sambar recipe, which we now eat regularly with rice at home.

Method

Heat oil in a pressure cooker.

Add chopped onions and tomatoes and fry for 2 minutes on high heat. Stir.

Drain water from the pre-soaked daal and add to the pressure cooker.

Add turmeric powder, salt and red chilli powder.

Fry for two minutes, and then add 2 cups water.

Pressure cook for 5 minutes on medium heat.

Turn off heat and cool, then open the cooker and mash the daal lightly.

Stage 2

String drumsticks and cut them into 2½-inch pieces.

Add ½ tsp salt + ½ tsp turmeric to drumstick pieces. Add water to just cover the drumsticks.

Let boil for 10-15 minutes till tender from inside (poke with a toothpick to check).

When done, add sambar powder and tamarind paste.

Boil once again without stirring.

As soon as it boils, add to the daal.

Add curry leaves and let the daal boil once more.

Stage 3

Put ½ tbsp oil in a shallow tempering (tadka) pan.

When hot, add the mustard seeds.

When the seeds start spluttering, break red chillies into 2 pieces each and add.

Pour this tadka on top of the sambar just before serving it.

10-minute Thoran

serves 4

Another one from Pinky, who says this southern bean thoran dish is the best one can conjure up. She experiments with various kinds of vegetables like carrots, cabbage and even bitter gourd.

Ingredients

1 tbsp + ½ tbsp vegetable oil
1 tsp mustard seeds (rai)
1 dry red chilli, broken in half
1 cup French beans, topped tailed and cut into 1" pieces
½ tsp salt
¼ cup coconut, grated
2 green chillies
10 curry leaves

Method

Grind the coconut, green chillies and curry leaves into a coarse paste and keep aside. Heat oil in a wok till the oil is smoking.

Add mustard seeds. Wait till they start spluttering and add the broken pieces of red chilli.

Quickly add the fresh green cut beans and toss nicely so that the mustard seeds are mixed well with the beans. Add salt.

Cover the wok, but every 45 seconds, toss the beans. Do this for around 4-5 minutes.

Keep checking the beans to ensure that they don't turn very dark or blackish, and retain their fresh green colour.

Remove the beans from the heat when firm yet tender and quickly mix in the coconut, chilli and curry leaf mixture.

Heat for 5 minutes.

Serve immediately.

Crispy Crackling
Bhindi

Super easy

serves 4-6

This bhindi is a favourite of ours, but each family seems to have its own variant. We love it for the crispy texture and the simplicity of the cooking method. This is my cousin Priti's recipe.

Ingredients

½ kg bhindi (okra or ladies' fingers)
1 tbsp + ½ tbsp oil
½ tsp cumin seed powder
½ tsp red chilli powder
1½ tsp coriander powder
1 tsp dried mango powder (amchur) (optional)
salt to taste

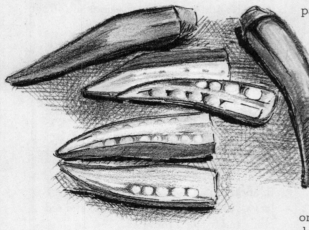

To add a slight tang you can add some amchur after the bhindi is fried, in which case you do not need to add the chaat masala before serving.

Method

Cut each bhindi lengthwise into 8 pieces.

Place a sheet of brown paper under a fan and spread the bhindi on it to dry for a few hours. Or you can just dry in the sun for 2 hours.

In a wok or handi, heat ½ cup oil.

When the oil is hot (check by putting one bhindi in, it should immediately rise to the surface), put the bhindi in a large metal sieve spoon (chhanni walla chammach) and immerse the entire chhanni in the oil.

When the bhindi is fried, remove the sieve and empty the bhindi onto an absorbent paper to remove the excess oil.

In a tadka ladle (which is essentially a ladle with a little bowl at the end) take 1 tsp oil, red chilli powder, coriander powder and salt and fry till masala is cooked. (This should take a minute.)

Pour on top of the bhindi. Serve hot with a sprinkle of chaat masala if you like.

If you have leftover bhindi, do not put in the fridge. Put it in a Tupperware box with the lid closed and leave it outside on your balcony overnight and use the next day. This will keep the bhindi crispy though not hot.

Heat the bhindi in a microwave before serving.

Hyderabadi Masoor Daal

While visiting a friend in Hyderabad, Priti was served this daal one evening. Since she doesn't enjoy daal at all, she tentatively had a spoon to be polite and was very pleasantly surprised at the delicious taste. She went on to help herself to copious amounts of it and says she pretty much 'drank' the daal that night.

Ingredients

1½ cups masoor daal, cleaned and washed
4 cups water
1 tsp turmeric powder (haldi)
salt to taste
1 dry red chilli
1½ tsp ginger garlic paste
1 tomato, chopped
2 green chillies, chopped
10 + 5 curry leaves
2 tbsp tamarind paste
2 tsp oil
1 tsp fresh ginger and garlic, chopped

Method

In a pressure cooker add the daal, water, turmeric and salt. Cover the cooker and set on medium heat.

After it whistles twice, cool and open the pressure cooker.

Leave the pressure cooker on the flame with the lid open and add the ginger garlic paste, tomato, green chilli, 10 curry leaves and tamarind paste and cook till daal is well mixed and slightly thick. (This should take 10-12 minutes.)

In another pan, heat 2 tsp oil, add 5 curry leaves, the chopped ginger garlic and red chilli and fry for 2 minutes.

Add this to the daal.

Serve immediately.

80-minute Kaali Daal

Easy peasy

serves 4-6

Ingredients

1 cup black urad daal
salt to taste
¼ cup ginger garlic paste
½ cup tomato puree, freshly made
3 tsp coriander powder (dhaniya)
1 tsp red chilli powder
2 tsp garam masala
½ cup cream
dollop of butter
sprig of coriander leaves

Arjun learnt how to make this daal when I visited him and he has added his own twist to it. It is the most requested dish by his friends in Geneva and the Philippines, and now, hopefully in Iran. This daal is tougher than other daals and does require to be soaked overnight in ample water. However, it still takes around 80 minutes to cook in a pressure cooker so be warned.

Method

Soak the daal overnight in ample water (the water should be one inch above the daal).

The next morning, drain the water and wash the daal thoroughly.

Put the daal in a pressure cooker.

Add enough water to cover the daal plus around 2 inches more.

Add the ginger garlic paste and salt and close the pressure cooker.

Cook over medium heat for 40 minutes.

Take off the heat and cool before opening the pressure cooker.

Add tomato puree, coriander, chilli and garam masala powder.

Close the pressure cooker and let this cook for another 40 minutes.

Once again, cool, then open the pressure cooker.

Add cream and dollop of butter, and also test for salt. If the salt is low, add some more salt and then close the pressure cooker.

Cook for 10 minutes.

Cool and then open the cooker and mash the daal a little.

Serve with finely chopped coriander leaves as a garnish.

Fragrant Sindhi Curry

My memories of Baby Didi or Sarojini, as she is formally known, had nothing to do with food. They were of this incredibly energetic older bhabhi who dressed in cool 'peddle-pushers' (it was the 1980s). While she never really entered the kitchen, she managed it perfectly well. With trepidation I asked her for a contribution to this book and she jumped up to offer me her version of a traditional Sindhi curry. She has played around with it by adding vegetables that she likes.

Ingredients

4 tbsp oil
¼ tsp cumin seeds (jeera)
¼ tsp white fenugreek seeds (safed methi)
4 tbsp chickpea flour (besan)
20 curry leaves
⅛ tsp asafoetida (hing)
¼ tsp red chilli powder
2-3 green chillies, chopped
1 tsp coriander leaves, chopped
1" ginger, chopped
2 potatoes, each cut in half with the skins on
8 French beans, threaded
4-5 ladies' fingers, cleaned well
2 yams cut into 2 each
1 carrot, roughly diced
1 cup dill, chopped (soya leaves)
5-6 kokums, soaked in water
2 tbsp tamarind paste
2 tomatoes, chopped
1 l water

Method

Heat oil in a large pot. When hot, add cumin seeds and white fenugreek seeds till you get the aroma of the cumin.

Add chickpea flour and stir on a high fire till it is golden brown and fragrant.

Add water. Keep stirring this mixture or the flour will get lumpy.

Add turmeric powder, curry leaves, green chillies, asafoetida and red chilli powder.

Keep stirring the mixture till it boils.

Add tomatoes, ginger, coriander leaves and green chillies and keep stirring.

Give this mix 2-3 hearty boils.

Add the potatoes, yam, French beans, dill and the carrot and salt to taste.

When the vegetables are half-cooked, add ladies' fingers, kokum and tamarind paste.

Cook till the vegetables are tender.

From Near and Far

The Sood family is fairly pan-Indian and global, not only geographically but also in the way they experiment and serve up food in their kitchens. And while some of them have stayed in states and countries where they say the food is nothing to write home about (and they don't), they do manage to use some local condiments and flavours in their food. Which leads to a wonderfully unique food experience.

Baked Tomato Spaghetti

serves 6-8

This pasta recipe has been in Joanna's family for years. (Joanna, an American of Italian descent, is my cousin Abhinav's wife.) She says she loves it just the way it is, with the chunks of baked tomatoes mixed in with the spaghetti. But she has had to adapt this recipe for Abhinav because he 'hates' tomatoes. He loves pasta sauce, salsa and many other things with tomatoes but he likes to pretend that those things don't have tomatoes and the key to this is that he can't see any large pieces! You can simply blend the roasted tomatoes in a mixer. Both versions are great. Problem solved!

Ingredients

12 tomatoes, ripe yet firm, medium-sized
6 large cloves garlic, minced
½ cup + ¼ cup parsley, chopped
2 tbsps + 2 tbsps + ¼ cup olive oil
450 g spaghetti
2 tbsp butter, room temperature
½ cup fresh basil, chopped
salt to taste
pepper to taste

Method

Cut tomatoes in half lengthwise and set cut-side up in a shallow 9" x 13" baking dish.

Sprinkle salt and pepper lightly on the tomatoes.

Mix garlic, ⅓ cup parsley and 2 tbsp oil in a bowl. Spoon mixture over the cut sides of the tomatoes.

Drizzle with 2 tbsp oil. Bake uncovered at 220°C for 60 minutes. Pan juices may become very dark but this is okay.

In a large, warm serving bowl, place butter, the remaining parsley, ¼ cup of oil, basil and the 4 halves.

Remove and discard most of the skin from the 4 baked tomato halves. Mash ingredients together.

Add cooked spaghetti and mix. Add the unused tomato halves and pan juices and mix gently. (At this point, you can choose to blend the tomatoes instead.)

Season with salt and pepper.

I-won't-cook Tagliatelle

Super easy

serves 6

When my cousin Geetanjalee got married, she told Deepak that she would never step into the kitchen, because she just didn't enjoy cooking. When I asked for her signature recipe, this is what she sent. I was very impressed with her until she told me that she didn't cook it of course, she just made her cook do it! Either way, it's still a lovely light veggie recipe.

Ingredients

375 g spinach pasta
25 g butter
200 g button mushrooms, sliced
1 lime, large (grated for zest, and juice squeezed)
200 ml cream
1 tsp pepper, freshly ground
1 tsp salt

Method

For the sauce:

In a frying pan, melt butter and fry the mushrooms and zest until the mushrooms have softened. This should take approximately 5 minutes.

Add the lime juice and seasoning and allow to bubble.

Slowly add cream and heat gently. (Do not bring to a simmer.) In 3 minutes you should have a nice creamy sauce.

For the pasta:

Bring 2 litres of water in a large pot to a rolling boil.

Add salt after the water boils (this helps water reach a higher temperature and also helps dissolve salt faster).

Put the pasta into the boiling water and stir gently for 2 minutes to help prevent it from sticking together. (Adding pasta after the water boils reduces mushiness.)

Cover and cook as per instructions on your pasta packet.

Test the pasta to ensure it is done: soft enough to eat but firm.

Using a colander, drain the water. (Pasta continues to cook even when taken off the heat, so drain quickly.)

Serve immediately with the mushroom lemon sauce and add freshly ground pepper.

Dushmani Chicken

Super easy   serves 4

Yes, you read it right. Dushmani it is. According to Rama maami, this was a dish taught to her by a lady who had a falling out with the rest of Rama maami's friends. Rama continued to make this dish for most parties, and her friends called it 'dushmani' or enemy's chicken. This dish was one of Rohit's favourites, especially with egg fried rice. We miss you both, Rama maami and Rohit.

Ingredients

1 kg boneless chicken, cut in chunks
1½ cups + 1 tbsp dark soya sauce
2 tbsp cornflour
¾ cup vegetable oil, for deep frying
¾ cup garlic, chopped
½ cup green chilli, chopped
½ cup spring onions, chopped
1 tbsp white vinegar

Method

Marinate the chicken in soya sauce for 45 minutes.

Add cornflour and mix well until the chicken is nicely coated.

Heat oil in a wok till it is ready for deep frying (you should see the vapour rising from the wok; test temperature by putting in a little cornflour paste, which should sizzle and fry immediately).

Deep fry the chicken in batches till it is golden brown.

Drain the fried chicken on kitchen paper.

Remove excess oil to leave only 2 tbsp in the wok.

Add garlic and sauté for a minute.

Add spring onions and sauté for a minute.

Add green chilli and sauté for a minute.

Put chicken back in the pan and sauté for a minute.

Add 1 tbsp soya sauce and vinegar. Stir to coat the chicken and fry on a high flame for 2 minutes.

Serve hot.

> *Rama maami said to me that one could experiment by adding chopped toasted cashew nuts or water chestnuts to this recipe.*

Weeknight Citrusy Chicken

serves 4

Ingredients

2 tbsp olive oil
250 g chicken, cleaned, without skin
2 cloves garlic, chopped
½ l orange juice, fresh or canned
3 tbsp lime or lemon juice
1 tsp salt
5 leaves basil, torn
1 orange, peeled, deseeded and cut into
thin roundels

*This is for me the simplest kitchen whip up,
when I am back from work late and really don't
want to cut, chop or do much mise en place.
The beauty of this recipe is that while easy
to throw together, its flavours are rich and
lip-smacking. It also looks fabulous garnished
with orange slices. It goes really well with a
simple baked potato and a side salad. I usually
end up making it at least once every few weeks.*

Method

In a non-stick pan, heat oil for 2 minutes.

Add garlic and stir for a minute till it
changes colour and releases a lovely
garlicky aroma.

Add the chicken pieces and stir well until
seared and slightly browned (this takes
4-5 minutes).

Remove the chicken from the pan and add
orange and lime juice along with salt.

Add basil. Heat the juices for 5 minutes and
add the chicken back to this sauce and cook for
10-12 minutes till the chicken is tender.

At this time, your sauce will be much thicker
and almost coat the chicken.

Add salt to taste.

Serve garnished with orange roundels.

Pepper Grilled Chicken

Rama maami was not just a great cook, but a cheerful one at that. I believe a person's personality translates into his or her food and Rama maami's food was as fanciful and elegant as she was. Her repertoire of recipes ranged from simple grills to fancy Lobster Thermidor. Here is one of our favourites: barbequed chicken. This is best eaten with garlic bread and a simple salad on the side.

Ingredients

½ kg chicken, boneless, cut in large chunks
1" piece ginger
8 cloves garlic
3 green chillies
8 cashew nuts
4 tbsp yogurt
2 tbsp cream
½ tsp + 2 tsp black pepper, freshly ground
½ tsp salt
1 capsicum, diced and seeds removed
1 onion, cut into large chunks
¼ cup pineapple chunks (from a tin)
2 tbsp olive oil
2 tsp butter

Method

In a mixer, grind together the ginger, garlic, green chilli, cashew nuts, yogurt, cream, pepper and salt.

Marinate the chicken in this paste for 2-3 hours.

Skewer the marinated chicken, onion cubes, capsicum squares and pineapple chunks.

Baste with a little oil and place on grill, turning occasionally till the chicken is cooked through and tender.

Remove the chicken and veggies from the skewer and keep aside.

In a pan, heat butter and add pepper.

Put the chicken in the pan with the pepper butter, heat and remove after 2 minutes.

Serve the chicken with capsicum, onions and pineapple.

Desi Lobster Thermidor

There was an old Calcutta restaurant, called the Sky Room, which my maamu Hari Om used to frequent for lunch with the family. The restaurant was famous for its Lobster Thermidor. After the Sky Room closed down, Hari Om had some of the chefs come and work in his home for a while, and that is how this recipe was perfected. It is by no means the traditional French recipe. Watch out for your arteries, though!

Ingredients

4 lobsters
4 l water
1 tsp salt
3 tbsp butter
100 g flour
1 clove garlic, minced
1 onion, chopped
250 g mushrooms
200 g cream
½ l milk
80 g gorgonzola cheese
4 tsp parsley, chopped

Method

Boil the lobster in a deep pot full of boiling water with salt for 9-10 minutes and transfer onto a tray to cool.

When cold, halve the lobster lengthwise into two pieces, starting from the tail, and remove the meat from inside. Crack the claws and do the same.

Remove all the meat and clean and preserve the lobster shell.

Dice the meat.

In a pan, heat butter, and when the butter bubbles, add flour.

Cook the flour till it changes colour to a deep brown.

Add garlic and onion and cook for 4 minutes.

Add mushrooms, cream and milk and stir constantly. Cook till the sauce is thickish.

Now add the lobster flesh and cook for 5 minutes in the sauce.

Arrange shells face up in a baking dish.

Carefully place meat and sauce in the halved lobster shells.

Top each with equal amounts of gorgonzola and parsley.

Bake in a preheated oven at 180°C for 10 minutes or till the cheese melts and the lobster mix is bubbling.

College Kung Pao

serves 4

While in college in USA and on a tight budget, Abhinav ended up at an 'all you can eat' Chinese buffet restaurant at least once a week. His roommates and friends joked that the food was so cheap because the kitchen used feral cats and stray dogs, to which he replied: They only added to the flavour! There was one dish that stood out, predominantly because of its spiciness: Kung Pao ... it was also one of the few dishes that hadn't been named after one of the Chinese leaders!

After he moved back to Delhi, Kung Pao was the one dish that he never found on any of the restaurant menus. Having tried ordering it at Tea House, the House of Ming and the Chinese cart by the side of the road near South Extension, it was decided that the only option left was to replicate it at home. After a few attempts, the recipe was fine tuned and made into a Sood Family regular.

Ingredients

2 boneless chicken breasts (you can also use lamb, shrimp, or beef)

For the marinade:
2 tsp soya sauce
2 tsp white wine or whisky
1 tbsp sesame oil
1½ tsp cornflour

For the sauce:
2 tbsp dark soya sauce
1 tbsp white wine or whisky
1 tsp sugar
2 tbsp red chilli sauce (sambal oelek and Sriracha chilli sauce mix preferred)
½ tsp sesame oil

For the rest:
8 dry red chilli peppers, small
2 cloves garlic, finely chopped
2 spring onions
2 tbsp vegetable oil + 2 tbsp vegetable oil
½ cup peanuts, unsalted, halved

Method

There are five steps to this: marinate the chicken, prepare the spicy sauce, stir fry the chicken, stir fry everything else, and mix the chicken back.

Cut the chicken into 1" cubes. Combine with the marinade ingredients, adding the cornflour last. Marinate for 25 minutes.

While the chicken is marinating, prepare the sauce and vegetables: In a small bowl, combine the dark soya sauce, whisky, chilli sauce, oil and sugar. Set aside.

Heat the wok over medium-high to high heat. Add 2 tbsp oil. When the oil is super hot, add the chicken. Stir fry for 7-10 minutes until it turns white and is pretty much cooked. Remove from the wok and drain the excess oil.

Cut the spring onions on the diagonal into thirds. To the same wok with the same drained oil, when the oil is really hot, add garlic and stir fry. Add red chilli peppers. Stir fry briefly until they turn dark red. Add the sauce to the wok. Bring to a boil.

Add the chicken back into the pan. Stir in peanuts and onions. Remove from heat and stir in the sesame oil. Serve hot.

Winter Swiss Fondue

This dish was, strangely enough, popular at home in Delhi and in Bangalore when we were kids. It became even more accessible when Arjun was living in Geneva and treated all of us who visited to a fondue dinner at the 400-year-old Café du Soleil (that claims to be the oldest restaurant in Geneva serving the best fondue in Switzerland) or, when that was fully booked, at Les Armures in the old city, that boasts (a bit too much) that it hosted Bill Clinton during his visit there. Fondue is a dish you either love or hate. Given that it's the national dish of Switzerland, the Swiss Tourism Board weighed in with their 'official version', and that is the basis of this recipe. While the debate on the best cheeses and recipes continues, fondue has become a winter staple at home in Delhi, especially with Peggy maami.

Ingredients

400 g Vacherin Fribourgeois cheese
400 g mature Gruyere cheese, grated
1¼ cups dry white wine
1 tbsp cornflour
1 garlic clove, minced
2 tbsp Kirsch (cherry liqueur)
⅛ tsp nutmeg
⅛ tsp black pepper
1 large baguette or other crusty white
loaf, cut into cubes

Method

In a fondue pot, combine both cheeses and heat until the cheese starts melting.

Separately, whisk together the wine and cornflour. Once the cheese has melted, stir the wine and cornflour mixture into the cheese in the fondue pot.

Bring to a boil, stirring continuously. Add the garlic, Kirsch, nutmeg and pepper.

Set the fondue pot's heat source to low to maintain a gentle simmer and place on the dining table.

Dip the bread cubes in the melted cheese and enjoy!

In a traditional cheese fondue, you can also add some herbs, finely sliced tomatoes or other ingredients that you think would add a preferred flavour. Gruyere is easily available. You may have trouble finding Vacherin Fribourgeois cheese. Consider substituting it with Fontina, Jarlsberg, Emmental or another good melting cheese. Using the right equipment in preparing and serving a fondue is critical. The fondue is best served in the same pot that it is cooked in. So it should be able to withstand a lot of heat. Else the cheese will solidify quickly. You also need large thin fondue forks. Arguably, the tastiest part of the fondue is the golden-brown toasted (not burnt) crusty cheese at the bottom of the pot that is scraped out and eaten. These shards are known as la religieuse (French for 'the nun').

Hangover Vodka Pasta

Easy peasy

serves 4

Hangovers run in our family. However, the older we grow, the more difficult and annoying our hangovers seem, especially if one has to work the next day. Despite all the caveats of filling one's stomach before drinking or lining the stomach with carbs and fatty foods, we always tend to feel we are infallible ... till the next morning. Abhinav is no stranger to hangovers. But for him, the morning after a drinking binge brings with it a double whammy. Not only does he get the usual headaches, he also gets ravenous. This recipe was concocted in the University of Connecticut, where, being a frat boy, hangovers were par for the course. A friend of his used to whip this up quickly for the gang. It was their lifesaver recipe and now it has become part of the weekly menu at home for him. (Because it is so-o-o good, not because he has a hangover every week.)

Ingredients

For the sauce:
3 chicken breasts, cubed
2 tbsp olive oil
1 onion, finely diced
8 cloves garlic, finely chopped
¼ cup tomatoes, diced
½ cup tomato puree
½ cup heavy full cream
2 shots of your favourite vodka
½ tsp salt
½ tsp black pepper
½ tsp red chilli
½ tsp dry oregano

For the pasta:
2 fists full of your favourite pasta (use 2 katoris for the smaller, less graspable versions)
1 tbsp olive oil
1 tsp salt
2 l water

Method

For the sauce:

In a large pan, heat olive oil.

Add the onion and chicken breast.

Just before the chicken becomes brown, add the garlic and let all of them brown together.

Fry till the chicken is cooked through.

Add the tomatoes, tomato puree, and full cream and bring the sauce to a boil.

Just as it starts to bubble, take the pan off the heat and add vodka and stir.

Add salt, pepper, red chilli powder and oregano to taste.

At this point the sauce should be slightly thick and should cling to the back of your wooden spatula.

For the pasta:

Bring 2 litres of water in a large pot to a roiling boil.

Add salt to the boiling water.

Put the pasta into the boiling water and stir gently for 2 minutes to help prevent pasta from sticking together.

Cover the pot and leave for 7 minutes or as per instructions on your pasta packet.

Test the pasta to ensure it's done. It should be soft enough to eat but firm.

Drain the water using a colander. Pasta continues to cook even when taken off the heat, so drain quickly. The pasta needs to be a little moist to absorb a slightly thick sauce like the one in this recipe.

After draining in the colander, move the pasta quickly to a serving bowl and serve immediately, else the pasta starts to get hard.

Garlic bread and a green salad are great side dishes when you want to make this a full meal.

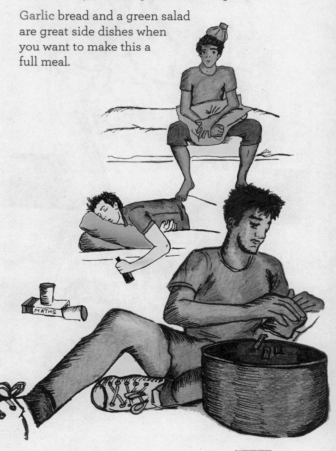

Naj Thai Green Curry

Easy peasy

serves 2

Bangkok is without doubt Arjun's favourite city, and authentic Thai food is certainly one of the main reasons he goes there. Yet, every time he eats Thai food in Thailand or elsewhere, he invariably orders Tom Kha Kai (a coconut chicken soup) and chicken in green curry. So much for diversity and new experiences! A few years ago, he took a cooking class at the Naj Thai Cooking School, a fantastic place in Silom that has its own herb garden and is operated by a brother-sister team with their mother. He loved the experience but he never got around to cooking Thai food using fresh ingredients himself. Eventually, when he moved to the Philippines, his cook, Long Long took up this challenge. She was so successful that he gained 15 kg in two years! Here are the recipes of Naj Cooking School for the chicken in green curry. Some of the ingredients are not easily found but you can substitute them. However, try not to substitute galangal with ginger; the tastes are completely different, they just belong to the same family.

Ingredients

For the green curry paste:
1 tsp coriander seeds
1 tsp cumin seeds
2 pieces shallot
3 pieces galangal
1 stalk lemongrass (use the bulb part)
2 pieces galingale (a yellow rhizome not to be confused with galangal)
1½ tsp shrimp paste
4 cloves garlic
6 green chilli spur pepper (the fat Thai chillies)
1 tbsp vegetable oil

For the curry:
100 g chicken breast, sliced
3 tbsp vegetable oil
2 cup coconut milk
4 green Thai aubergine, small, diced
40 g Thai aubergine, diced
4 tbsp yard-long beans, chopped (called chori in Hindi, barboti in Bengali)
6 kaffir lime leaves
1½ tbsp fish sauce
3 tsp palm sugar
1 tsp sugar
1 tsp salt
5 leaves Thai sweet basil
2 tsp Thai red chillies, slit lengthwise

Method

For the green curry paste:

Heat a pan to a low temperature.

Add coriander and cumin seeds, stirring till fragrant.

Remove from heat and grind together in mortar, remove and keep aside.

In the mortar, grind together shallot, galangal, lemongrass, galingale, shrimp paste, garlic and green chilli spur pepper till nicely blended into a paste.

Mix the paste and powder together.

Add vegetable oil in a pan.

Stir in the paste and cook for 5-6 minutes.

Remove from heat and keep the paste aside.

For the curry:

Warm a large pan over medium heat. Add oil and swirl it around the pan.

Add the green curry paste and stir rapidly till fragrant and then slowly add coconut milk.

Stir for 2-3 minutes till you see a film of green oil on the curry surface.

Add the chicken pieces, stirring well. When the curry boils, reduce heat to a simmer.

Add the green Thai aubergines, Thai aubergine, yard-long beans, kaffir lime leaves and simmer for 3 minutes till the veggies are softened yet firm and colourful.

Add fish sauce, palm sugar, sugar and salt and simmer for 4-5 minutes.

Remove from the heat and add basil leaves and red chilli.

PHO
pronounced
Fuh

Easy peasy

serves 2-3

To rhyme with 'Huh', which is the reaction I had when I was told how to say the word. Not pho or fo or fah. Fuh! I started making this soup last winter after having a hot bowl of it at the Commonwealth mela (Vietnam at the Commonwealth mela brought on another 'huh?', but hey, I got a great soup) and it literally chased away an oncoming fever. I have a feeling the Sriracha has a lot to do with it.

Pho is a hearty, healthy, inexpensive street food soup in Vietnam. Instead of the typical raw beef version, on which they just pour hot soup, I went desi and used chicken. Be warned though, this is not a soup you can just whip together last minute at home. You need a few ingredients that really make this soup pop and some of them are not commonly available.

Ingredients

150 g boneless chicken, cubed or sliced long
2 cups stock (see page 80)
2 tsp chilli oil or olive oil
50 g spring onions, chopped
1" ginger, chopped
2 star anise
1 cinnamon
3 tsp fish sauce (if you don't have it, don't bother, just another of my variations!)
1 tsp salt
2 tsp garam masala
2 bird-eye chillies, sliced lengthwise, seeds removed
100 g rice noodles (the thinnest white ones in packets that are sold as Thai rice noodles here)
½ cup bean sprouts (the white long Chinese ones, not the sprouted daal we have for breakfast)
⅓ cup peanuts, crushed lightly
a handful of coriander leaves, basil and mint, chopped
2 eggs, hard boiled and sliced into concentric circles
2 limes, cut in quarters
1 onion, sliced long and deep fried till crispy
Sriracha sauce (this is a must have, and you can use it in a lot of recipes when you want to add a dash of chilli)
1 onion, sliced long and deep fried till crispy

Method

Heat oil in a saucepan for 2 minutes.

When the oil is hot, add spring onions, ginger, star anise, cinnamon and let them cook for 2 minutes on a high flame.

Add sliced chicken and cook for 5 minutes till it turns a little beige-brown.

Add the stock with fish sauce, garam masala and salt (I add 1 tsp dried shrimp here since it really adds a punch to the flavour, but this is purely optional).

Cook for 8-11 minutes or till the chicken is tender.

Add sliced chillies just before taking the Pho off the fire.

Remove the star anise and cinnamon from the soup mixture.

In a separate bowl, place the rice noodles and pour boiling water from a kettle onto it and let it sit for 9-11 minutes. This is how long it will take to cook. When it's done, drain the water.

For the assembly:
Now you need to start assembling the soup bowls. Here's the part where you can be artistic and make it look all pretty and exciting.

Start by dividing the rice noodles into equal portions, one for each bowl, so they go right at the bottom.

Pour the Pho on top of this till the bowl is ⅔ full, ensuring there are enough chicken pieces too.

Divide the soup (in your head) into 5 equal parts – pretend the top of the soup bowl is a circular pie and your teacher has told you to divide the circle into 5 pieces.

Now, in each piece beautifully arrange the following on top of the soup: bean sprouts, peanuts, assorted chopped herbs, egg slices, lime quarters, crispy onions.

Serve with Sriracha sauce on the side, so that you can add as much as you need. You can even slice a bird-eye chilli and add it on top for effect. This Pho not only looks beautiful but tastes incredible too.

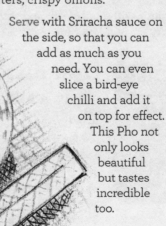

20-minute
Chicken, Many Ways

Super easy

serves 2

Just like I always have stock on hand to make soup (see page 80), I also always have chicken. Before I leave the house in the morning, I get the cook to defrost the chicken and marinate it in 1 cup hung yogurt, ginger and garlic. With this basic marinade there are so many easy ways I can make chicken in 20 minutes when I get back home. I keep freshly made Thai paste and pesto frozen in individual packets for an easy defrost. I always keep a jar of gongura pickle (a typically Andhra leaf pickle) and a box of zataar (a Mediterranean herb mix) too. Keep in mind that these are not traditional and 'accurate' recipes. They are my quick fixes for a quick dinner and they taste just as good.

Default marinade

Marinate 2 chicken breasts or legs in ½ cup yogurt, 1 tbsp each of ginger and garlic with 1 tsp of salt and 1 tsp red chilli powder.

Gongura chicken

Add the chicken to pan and cook till the marinade is dry (it should take about 5 minutes), add 2 tbsp gongura pickle. Fry or bake till done (approximately 10-15 minutes) and serve. Garnish with 5 curry leaves.

Tandoori chicken

Simply put in a preheated gas tandoor or oven at 180°C for 15-17 minutes and serve with onion rings and lime.

Thai-flavoured chicken

Add the chicken to the pan and cook till marinade is dry. Add half a cup of Thai green paste (recipe on page 66), 1 tsp salt and cook till done. Garnish with lime slices and serve.

Pesto chicken

Add the chicken to a pan and cook for 5 minutes till the marinade is dry. In a mixer whizz together a bunch of basil leaves (30-40) with 25 g pine nuts and 3 cloves garlic and 1 tsp salt. Add this to the chicken and cook till done.

Lebanese-style chicken

Add 2 tsp zataar, 1 tsp salt, 2 crushed garlic cloves and the juice of one lime to the chicken and grill in a preheated tandoor or oven (180°C) for 15-17 minutes. Serve with preserved lemons if you have some or with lime.

Light and Healthy

Many people I know go on a 'healthy food' binge from time to time. Whether to just feel better or lose weight or to detox, you will find in this section simple and compound salads, some hearty soups and lightly poached and steamed food.

Hanoi-inspired Salad

Super easy serves 2

My cousin Ayesha chanced upon this salad in Vietnam while walking around the Latin Quarter. She ordered it only because it was too hot a day to eat a traditional Pho (see page 68 for a recipe). She feels it is the perfect example of Vietnamese food culture and history, combining the refined preparation and method of French cooking with the strong yet balanced flavours of the East. She says the most important part of this dish is the preparation because the salad needs to stand up on the plate and not flop over. It can be served as a main course or on the side with beef or seafood to make it a whole meal.

Ingredients

The salad

1 Chinese cabbage (the one with an elongated head)
2 spring onions
1 red pepper
5 rocket leaves
2 tbsp pine nuts, toasted
5 basil leaves
5 mint leaves
2 cloves garlic
5 banana flowers (if available)
1 mango or 5 lychees (optional)

The dressing:

Mix together
2 tsp sesame oil
1 tsp fish oil
2 red chilles, sliced lengthwise
1 tsp brown sugar (if using fruit in the salad)
2 limes, juiced

Method

Prepare the vegetables as follows:
Chinese cabbage: Julienne the stem and chop the leaf.
Spring onions: chop the stem and the bud.
Julienne the red pepper.
Tear the rocket leaves by hand into bits.
Tear the mint leaves and basil leaves by hand into bits.
Using a mandoline, very carefully slice the garlic into thin chips. Heat oil in a pan and when hot, dunk the garlic into it for a few seconds to make into chips. Remember, if it is cooked longer, it will burn and we don't want that.
If using fruit, dice into 2-cm cubes.

Mix all these ingredients together with the dressing and prop up on the plate so it stands tall.

Garnish with banana flowers.

Serve immediately.

Tomato & Bocconcini
Salad with Kasundi

Super easy

serves 4

Ingredients

250 g ripe but firm tomatoes
50 g bocconcini (I use the one by Flanders)
1½ tbsp mustard oil + 1½ tbsp extra virgin olive oil.
4 tbsp apple cider vinegar
1 red chilli, slit lengthwise
2 tbsp kasundi
1 tsp salt
½ tsp pepper
5 basil leaves, shredded

Exhausted with the traditional Tomato Mozzarella salad on every menu and every dinner, I tried my hand at mixing and matching a few ingredients. I used bocconcini (mini egg-sized mozzarella cheeses) instead of slicing mozzarella and added kasundi to the dressing. Today, this salad is a 5-minute whip-up at home. My real validation came from my eight-year-old niece who tasted this and said, 'Bua, you make the best food ever.' She must have been Bengali in her past life.

Method

In a small screwtop jar, add oil, vinegar, red chilli, kasundi, salt and pepper.

Shake well till the oil and vinegar are emulsified (blended well). Store in the fridge till ready to use. (I make this at least half an hour before the meal so that the flavours really blend with each other.)

Slice the top and bottom end off the tomatoes and dice them into 1" quarters. Put into a bowl.

Cut the bocconcini into quarters and add to the bowl.

Add the shredded basil leaves.

Now add the dressing a little at a time and keep tossing. (Do not smother the tomatoes with the dressing; they should be lightly coated.)

Serve immediately with warm crusty bread on the side.

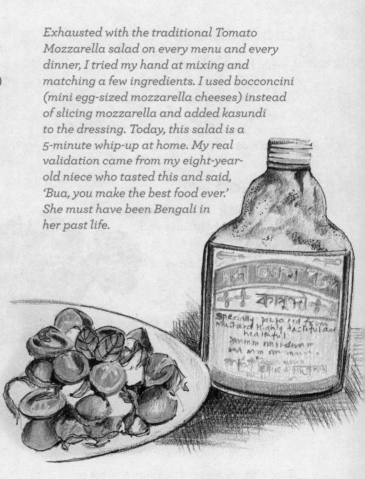

The Secret Broccoli Salad

Ingredients

1 small broccoli head
1 cup eggless mayonnaise
1 tsp garam masala
2 tsp Dijon mustard
8 dates, deseeded, chopped
¼ cup roasted peanuts

This is Seema's supposedly secret recipe which, according to her mother-in-law, and my Nimma maasi, she never shares with anyone. It is a favourite in the Kapur house. Whenever we visit, this is always the dish of choice. It can be served cold in the summer and, with a slight variation, hot in the winter. It's very quick to make and also very nutritional.

Method

Add the garam masala and Dijon mustard to mayonnaise and mix well.

Add the chopped dates into this mixture.

Stir and cool in the fridge.

Blanch the broccoli in a pot of boiling water for 2 minutes.

Let the broccoli cool in the fridge.

Just before serving, take the broccoli out of the fridge and break it into florets or roughly dice it.

Add the cool sauce on top of it. Put enough so it is completely covered.

Top with the roasted peanuts and serve.

Seema says this can be made in a slightly different fashion if you want a warm version. After you blanch the broccoli, take a pan and add a glob of butter to it. Add a handful of sliced almonds and 2 whole dry red chillies. Wait till almonds are toasted and then add the blanched warm broccoli to this butter sauce. Serve immediately.

Slimming Hummus

Ingredients

1 cup dry chickpeas (kabuli chana),
soaked overnight
2 tbsp tahini sauce
2 limes, juiced
2 garlic cloves
salt to taste
2 tsp red chilli powder or zataar
(a Lebanese herb mix)
3 tbsp olive oil

Method

Pressure cook chickpeas with enough
water till overdone. If you are using canned
chickpeas, add as is.

Blend the boiled chickpeas and garlic to
make a smooth paste.

Add tahini sauce and continue blending.

Add lime juice to taste and mix with a ladle.

Add salt and check for taste.

Serve in a bowl and put ample zataar on the
top as a garnish. Top with a little olive oil in
the centre.

Serve with warm pita bread or lavash (a thin
bread from Iran and Turkey) triangles, or
even with crudités.

*This is a favourite with my cousin Priya's
friends and she is well known for this recipe.
It's a great low-fat dip, high in fibre, full of
protein and calcium. You can even use it
instead of mayo on your sandwiches.*

*You can also add various flavours to the
hummus: fresh chopped coriander while
blending the chickpeas to make this a nice
coriander hummus. Add a little garam
masala as a garnish to give it that Indian
touch instead of zataar. Or use sun-dried
tomotoes while whisking or even cheese
and chives for a creamier fatty dip.*

75

Fish en Papillote

Easy peasy

serves 4

I made this fish when we got ourselves a gas tandoor. I experimented a couple of times and hit upon a light and easy recipe which was Asian flavoured and worked well with this en papillote-steamed style. I purchased parchment paper from USA (you don't get it easily here) and followed a YouTube video on how to seal the en papillote parcel, and what emerged was a light flavourful recipe.

Ingredients

4 fish fillets (I prefer Sea Bass)
1 + 2 limes, juiced
1 lime, sliced thin
½ cup coriander leaves
2" ginger
2 stalks lemongrass
4 cloves garlic
2 green chillies
2 onions, medium-sized, thinly sliced into roundels
2 heads bok choy, trimmed and chopped
coarse salt and freshly ground pepper

Method

Clean and rub the fish with juice of 1 lime and leave for 30 minutes.

Blend coriander, ginger, lemongrass, garlic, chillies to make a paste.

Take a parchment sheet and fold it diagonally in half.

Place some of the paste in front of the diagonal crease and place the fish on top of it. Add more paste on top of the fish, about a tsp.

Top the fish with bak choy, lime slices and concentric circles of onions.

Add a little salt.

Fold the other half of the parchment over and crease and fold the edges to seal the fish.

It will now look like a crescent-shaped packet.

Make 4 such packets and place in a preheated tandoor or oven (180°C) for 10-12 minutes till the parchment puffs up.

Serve carefully, making sure you let the steam escape from the side without burning your face or hands.

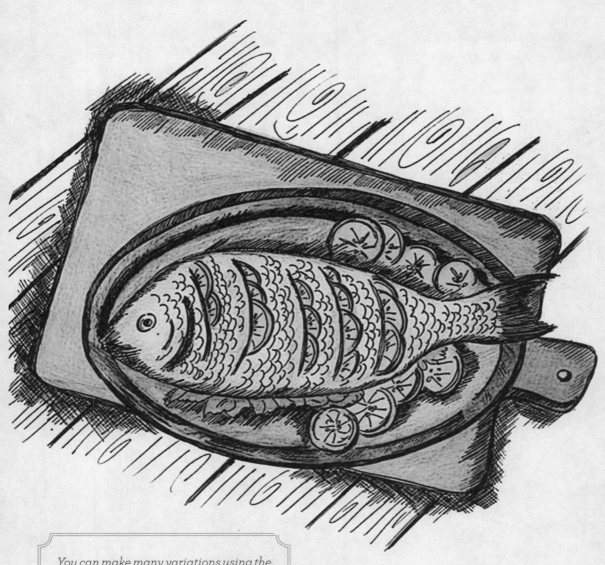

You can make many variations using the
above method. Substitute tomato sauce
(see page 105) instead of the green paste
and top with sliced onions and capers.

When under the weather

'I need pampering.'

'No, I really don't feel like eating anything. My mouth tastes sour. Everything tastes flat.'

'Toast? Gross. Can't I get something else instead?'

'I have a hangover, and I've already had two Alka Seltzers.'

Sounds familiar?

Well, we have all at some time or the other been in the throes of a fever, a racking cough and cold, with a terribly leaky nose (probably adding nicely to the bottom line of Kleenex), or experienced an incredible hangover. It's at times like these that food seems so unimportant. And is so important.

Living alone without much help or a loving partner who cooks is tough when ill. For me, sick food means any of the following things: khichdi (mild on the stomach and slides easily down your oesophagus); soup (hot, steaming, comfort for the throat); and sometimes curd rice (I have it even on regular days).

I also consider having a hangover being ill, so I have my hangover recipe for you too.

Stock

Easy peasy

The base for all my soups is a nice hearty stock. You should always have home-made stock in your freezer. (Even though some of my aunts use readymade soup cubes as a base, I do not like to do so since they are loaded with preservatives and salt. And that defeats the purpose of feeling better and healthier.) Forget Larousse Gastronomeique recipes and the other ultra-complicated French methods of making stock. Here is what I do which works just as well. The one piece of kitchen equipment I can't do without is my stock pot. Since I make my stock once a week, this is essential for my soup cooking. Try and buy a stock pot with a nice heavy base and a tight lid. Making stock takes a couple of hours so make it when you are in between chores at home. This will allow you to keep an eye on the stock.

This recipe will give you enough stock to last for 16 cups of soup. I divide them into 10x2 portion Tupperware cups and freeze them. Whenever I need to make soup I pop a cup out of the freezer, defrost quickly in the microwave and am all set to get cracking.

Ingredients

1 kg chicken bones, washed and cleaned
2 large onions, quartered
4 carrots, roughly diced (large-uneven will do)
4-6 ribs of celery (if they are in season)
1 leek (if it is in season)
2 bay leaves, dry (tejpatta)
8-10 peppercorns
2 cloves garlic, peeled
18 cups water

Method

Place the chicken bones, vegetables and spices in your stockpot.

Turn the heat up and lightly roast the veggies and bones for 3-4 minutes till the bones start getting a little colour. If it's a vegetarian stock, roast for 6-7 minutes.

Add the water (the water should be at room temperature).

Cook on high heat. You will start seeing little bubbles breaking through the stock liquid.

Turn the heat down to medium and let the stock simmer gently. At this point, you will start seeing a cloudy scum rise to the surface as bubbles or as a messy bunch of particles.

Using a very fine sieve spoon or slotted spoon, gently skim the surface and throw the scum away. (You may need to skim the surface every ten minutes or so for the first 60 minutes.)

After this you can cover the lid and let the stock simmer for at least 2-3 hours so that the flavours of the bones, veggies and spices really seep in.

Pour the stock out into a big bowl using a cheesecloth so that not only are the veggies and solids strained, but so is the scum.

Throw away the bones, the unusable veggies and the scum.

Cool the stock and divide it up into little bowls of 2 portions each, seal the Tupperware and pop into the freezer.

Chicken Rasam

Easy peasy

serves 2

Let's start with my all-time favourite:
Chicken Rasam. It's hot, it's spicy, it's easy to
whip up and it gets my sinuses going quick.

I spent a large part of my childhood in
Bangalore and rasam was par for the course.
After I moved back to Delhi, the rasam
available here felt not only ghastly to taste
but also unappealing to look at. And then I
discovered Dakshin at the ITC and had their
chicken rasam. Bangalore only ever offered
me traditional vegetarian rasam. I had
never come across a non-veg rasam. I was
so blown away by the amazing flavour that
I decided to start experimenting with the
soup and finally I came up with a concoction
that works for me. While you will find tons of
recipes that require you to grind fresh rasam
powder and other ingredients, I prefer to
keep it simple. I make the soup almost every
week in winter and it really helps when I feel
the beginnings of a sore throat or am a bit
under the weather. Keep in mind that I prefer
things sour, so my slant is that way. You can
adjust the flavours to suit your taste.

Ingredients

2 tsp vegetable oil (I use olive oil)
150 g boneless chicken breast, cubed
2 tsp toor daal
½ tsp turmeric powder (haldi)
2 garlic cloves, chopped (or ½ tsp
garlic paste)
1 onion, medium-sized, chopped
5-7 curry leaves
3 tomatoes, medium-sized and somewhat
firm, roughly chopped
2 cups stock (see page 80)
1 tsp rasam powder (for those who prefer
making it themselves, there are lots of
variations on the net you can experiment
with; I just use MTR)
3 stalks coriander leaves, chopped (or 4 tsp
coriander leaves)
1 lime, juiced
salt to taste

Method

Use a small pressure cooker (if you have one). Set it on a medium flame with a little bit of oil to coat the bottom. For those who don't have a cooker, follow the same steps in a saucepan, but instead of 5 minutes in the cooker, simmer the chicken till tender and daal is cooked (use a lid on your saucepan).

When the oil is hot, add garlic, onion, curry leaves, daal and turmeric powder.

When the onion is slightly translucent, add the chicken and let it sear and change colour. This should take 3-4 minutes.

Add tomatoes and cook for another 2 minutes, till you see the tomatoes are also changing colour and becoming darker.

At this point, add the stock, rasam powder and some salt (use just 1 tsp to start with) and mix well.

Put the lid on the pressure cooker, set the flame on high and let be for around 5 minutes. (Don't cook longer thinking you need to suck the nutrients out of the chicken. Remember we are already using a nice concentrated stock. All we need is for the boneless pieces to become tender and the daal to cook.)

Turn the flame off, let the pressure cooker stand till all the pressure has been released and then open the lid.

At this point, taste the soup. If it's sour enough from the tomatoes, leave it, but if you feel it needs a little tang, add the lime juice. Also adjust the salt at this point. Do this after you have added the lime juice.

With the lid off the cooker, start the fire again, throw in the chopped coriander leaves and simmer the soup for 2-3 minutes.

Serve immediately.

Amla Soup

Easy peasy   serves 2

This is a great one for colds and runny noses and surprisingly, even for upset stomachs. It gives you a super shot of Vitamin C. It is similar to the rasam recipe, with just a few changes to get the amla in. The amla makes for a slightly bitter aftertaste but it's very light in flavour because of the stock and daal. And ever so healthy.

Ingredients

4 amla
1 cup + 1 cup chicken stock (see page 80)
salt to taste
¼ cup toor daal
2 tsp olive oil
4 peppercorns
1 onion, medium-sized, chopped
2 garlic cloves, chopped (or ½ tsp garlic paste)
½ tsp turmeric powder (haldi)
1 spoon tamarind paste
½ tsp rasam powder
1 tomato, medium-sized and somewhat firm, roughly chopped
5-7 curry leaves
3 stalks coriander leaves, chopped (or 4 tsp coriander leaves)

Method

In a pressure cooker add the 4 amla cut into quarters with about 1 cup of the stock. Add ½ tsp salt, the daal and let it cook for 5-7 minutes on a medium flame till the amla is soft and mushy.

Remove from the heat.

When cool, open. Using your fingers, smash the amla in the stock and remove the seeds.

In a saucepan, heat oil for 2 minutes.

When hot, add peppercorns, onions and garlic and heat till they change colour.

Add turmeric powder, salt, tamarind paste, rasam powder and the extracted pulp of the amla including the stock liquid, and cook for a minute.

Add the balance stock, tomato and curry leaves and put it all to boil for a good 5 minutes.

Taste at this point and add salt or more tamarind if you need.

Add the coriander, heat for a minute and then serve.

Karela Soup

Easy peasy

serves 2

No, don't skim past this one. It is not as gross as you think. Not only is karela a great blood purifier, but it also helps patients with diabetes. It is also a great metabolism booster, so if you are feeling tired and sluggish, this will help. And anyway, when you are sick and your mouth feels sour, will you notice the difference? So just make it and do a bottoms up. You might be surprised.

Ingredients

2 bitter gourds (karela)
2 tsp oil
⅛ tsp asafoetida (hing)
4 peppercorns
½ tsp turmeric (haldi)
salt to taste
1 tsp cumin seeds (jeera)
½ tsp black mustard seeds (rai)
2 onions, chopped
2 tsp jaggery powder
1 tsp tamarind paste
2 cups stock (see page 80)
1 tsp coriander leaves, chopped

Method

Wash and peel the karela and then slit it lengthwise from end to end. Pull it open and discard all the seeds. Slice the karela widthwise into ½" strips.

In a pan, heat the oil.

Add peppercorns, hing, turmeric, jeera and mustard seeds. Wait till the seeds pop but don't let the masala burn.

Now add the onions and let them turn translucent.

Add the karela and stir fry for 3 minutes.

Add jaggery powder, tamarind paste and salt. This will make your pan a bit sticky, so you can add a spoon or two of the stock to keep the masala from sticking to the bottom of the pan. Fry for a couple more minutes.

Add the stock (use the vegetarian version).

Cook on a medium flame covered with a lid for 15 minutes (this gives the karela enough time to seep into the stock).

Remove the lid and sample just the liquid part of the soup. It should taste slightly bitter with subtle undertones of jaggery and tamarind.

If you need to add more salt, do and let it boil for a minute longer.

Remove from the fire and strain the liquid so that the spices and the karela pieces are no longer in the soup and it is clear.

Serve hot, garnished with coriander leaves.

Geeli Khichdi

Easy peasy

serves 2

Ingredients

1 cup yellow moong daal (without skin)
1 cup rice
1 tsp salt
5 cups water
2 tsp ghee
½ tsp cumin seeds (jeera)

Method

Soak rice and daal together for half an hour, then drain.

In a pressure cooker add water, daal, rice and salt.

Close the cooker and cook on high heat.

After 1 whistle (it literally sounds like a whistle unless your cooker is faulty), simmer for 7-8 minutes.

Take off the heat. When the cooker is cool and there is no pressure left, open cooker and transfer the khichdi into a serving bowl.

Now the yummy part – the chhonk or tadka with pure fatty ghee ... yum!

Take a big ladle, put ghee in it and place on a high flame. Add cumin seeds and when they splutter, quickly pour over the khichdi. The khichdi is now ready to be served.

You can garnish with coriander leaves if you want to make it prettier. (I do.)

Serve with kachumber salad.

Sookhi Khichdi

Easy peasy serves 2

Ingredients

2 cups rice
1 cup moong daal, with skin on
1½ tsp salt
½ tsp cumin seeds (jeera)
2 tsp ghee
6 cups water
4 whole black peppercorns
4 cloves

Method

Soak rice and daal together for half an hour, then drain.

In a pressure cooker, heat ghee.

When hot, add cumin, black pepper and cloves. When the cumin seeds splutter, add daal and rice and fry for 2 minutes.

Add water and salt to taste, and close the cooker.

Turn the flame up high and wait for the pressure cooker to whistle once.

Reduce heat to medium. After 5 minutes take off the heat and let the cooker stand for 5 minutes.

Open the pressure cooker and remove the khichdi.

It will now appear dry with the daal really looking like it is blooming.

No ghee on this one, folks, this is a low-fat version.

Garnish with coriander.

Spiced Buttermilk

serves 2

Here's another great little drink, light with fresh flavours, to have when under the weather. This is from Pinky's repertoire.

Ingredients

1½ cup yogurt
2 curry leaves
rind from a quarter of a lime
(use a soft lime)
¼" ginger, grated
3 cups water
4 cubes ice

Method

Blend yogurt, curry leaves, lime rind, water and ice till the ice is completely crushed. Garnish with ginger.

There is no need for salt, but if you feel you can't do without it, add some.

> *Pinky sometimes adds a tadka/ tempering by heating ½ tsp oil in a small frying pan, spluttering some mustard seeds, and then pouring on the buttermilk.*

Cool Curd Rice

Super easy

serves 2

This is a great dish for an upset stomach. Pinky says it is also used in south India to help cool your 'insides'. I eat it on days when I don't have an appetite and I just mix a yummy spicy pickle with it. It's not meant to be a simple curd-mixed-with-rice dish (as most of us northies feel); it uses milk too. This gives it a slightly wet and mushy texture, which really works. This dish has to be eaten cold. Make it in the morning, so you can eat it for lunch or dinner. If you want to take it to work, you get these great little insulated boxes that keep food at the right temperature.

Ingredients

1 katori short, thick rice (do not use basmati for this dish)
¾ kg yogurt (curd)
½ cup milk
1 tsp black mustard seeds
1 dry red chilli, broken into 4 pieces
1 tsp oil
10 curry leaves
2 green chillies, chopped
1" ginger, chopped
salt to taste

Method

Cook the katori of rice till it is done.

Mash it slightly.

In a separate pot, mix yogurt and milk. Add salt and whip the mixture.

Heat oil in a small pan for the tadka or tempering. Add mustard seeds and red chilli.

When the mustard splutters, add curry patta, ginger and green chillies.

Add this tadka to the yogurt mixture and mix nicely.

By this time, the rice should have cooled. When it is lukewarm, add the yogurt mixture and mix well with the rice.

Refrigerate for a minimum of 2 hours before serving.

Hangover Heaver

Super easy

serves 1-2 depending on how ravenous you are

I truly suffer when I have a hangover. (Conventional wisdom recommends abstinence, a glass of water for every glass of alcohol, and other such boring stuff to avoid hangovers. But of course, I just choose to suffer.) Over years of experimenting and after reading lots of articles on ingredients that might help your body, I discovered eggs were a big help, so were chillies. I quickly decided I would alter my regular omelette to accommodate chillies (I have very low tolerance for them otherwise). I have this with crispy toast and white butter and a Virgin Mary spiked with lots of Tobasco and lime. It really helps ... or so I believe.

Ingredients

3 egg whites
1 tbsp butter (I use white)
½ cup onion, chopped
1 tomato, chopped
1 tsp green chillies, chopped
3 tbsp cream cheese (you can use a regular cream cheese)
¼ cup processed meat, chopped (use ham or turkey slices or chicken if you have any)
2 tsp fresh coriander, chopped

Method

Whip the egg whites till they are nice and fluffy. The trick is to aerate the eggs well. So lift your whisker in and out of the bowl in a marching movement while beating the eggs.

Heat butter in an omelette pan (this could be your fancy semicircular one or a regular 8-inch, round non-stick).

Add onions and sauté for a few minutes.

Add tomatoes and chillies and sauté for 3 minutes on a high flame till the liquid dries up.

Add eggs and, a minute later, add cheese and meat on top of the still liquidy egg mixture.

Flip the omelette if you have the mental agility or the skill at the time. If you are really hungover, just turn it into scrambled eggs, forget the artistry.

While still soft, slide it onto a crispy piece of toast and serve with a Virgin Mary spiked with pepper, salt, Worcestershire sauce, Tobasco and lime (all to your taste).

Teas that Heal

serves 2

Everyone has a couple of brews at home which are concocted double quick when one has a sore throat or a cold. Here are two very effective ones. If had several times a day, they help keep sore throats and colds at bay.

Cough and Cold Khaada

Ingredients

1 piece cinnamon
5 black peppercorns
4 cloves
1 bay leaf, dry (tejpatta)
8 leaves holy basil (tulsi)
1 tsp cumin seeds (jeera)
1 tsp carom seeds (ajwain)
½ tsp coriander seeds (dhaniya)
1" ginger, chopped
1" licorice root (if you have it)
2 cups water

If this is a little too sharp for your taste, add half a spoon of honey, although I force myself to have it as it is, every couple of hours.

Method

Boil water and add all these ingredients.

Continue boiling for 20 minutes.

Strain and serve.

Adrak ki Chai

serves 1

Ingredients

1 cup water
1½ tsp sugar
1 tsp tea leaves (the best mix is half spoon Darjeeling long leaf and half spoon Assam CTC)
1" ginger
½ cup hot milk

Method

Crush the ginger in a mortar and pestle. Keep the pulp and juice separately in a small bowl.

Boil water, milk and sugar together. Add the tea leaves and as soon as it comes to a boil again, turn the flame off.

Add crushed ginger and juice and cover the tea, and let stand for 2-3 minutes to let the ginger seep in.

Serve piping hot. (I don't strain the crushed ginger out of this, but you could.)

6

Anytime Eats

Some familiar, some new, some crunchy. Little and big eats that you can munch on pretty much any time of the day.

Crunchy elephant ears

Somewhat easy   serves 4

A few months ago, my nieces Aradhana and Arianna decided to make their favourite Arbi patta rolls or pataud as they are more commonly known. I was a willing partner in the endeavour. We had just received a supply of the giant-sized leaves called colocasia leaves, elephant ears or taro leaves. While we made the mixture to use in the rolls, we added a little tamarind paste and it turned the gooey besan paste a somewhat strange colour. Of course, five-year-old Arianna piped up and said, 'Bua, that looks like poo-poo. Are we making poo-poo pattas?' Since this evoked a giggle from me (big mistake), she started like a stuck record: 'Are we making poo-poo pattas? Will we eat poo-poo pattas?' We did make the pataud amidst a lot of shushing and hushing and giggling – it's one of the big favourites with the family at snack time. Arbi leaves can be grown at home in a pot and when not in season, I use spinach leaves as a poor substitute.

Ingredients

12 large arbi leaves
100 g chickpea flour (besan)
salt to taste
½ tsp red chilli powder
½ tsp garam masala
1 tbsp tamarind paste/dry pomegranate
seeds or dried mango powder
1 tsp black cumin seeds
1 cup vegetable oil (optional, to fry)

Method

Mix the chickpea flour, chilli powder, cumin, garam masala and tamarind paste with some water till it forms a nice thick paste. (Don't forget the cumin; it actually prevents the bitter taste of the leaves from catching in your throat.)

Chop the extended stems off the arbi leaves.

Lay the arbi leaf as flat as you can with the front face down.

On a clean flat surface, try and lay one arbi leaf face down and spread the besan mixture on it. Place another leaf on top of it, overlapping the first by at least 1". Do the same with a third leaf. What you now have is a vertical line of 3 leaves overlapping with each other with the besan paste on it.

Add another layer of arbi leaves almost exactly on top of this (again face down) and cover this layer of three also with besan paste. Repeat this 2 more times to form a four-layer deck of leaves.

Since the leaves are not rectangular, carefully fold the pointy part of the leaves 1" towards the centre, and press down. Do the same with the opposite edge of the leaves (fold in 1" towards the centre).

Start rolling (like a Swiss roll) all the 4 sets of leaves carefully into a tight cylinder, starting from the edge closest to you. It will look like a leaf log.

Tie this with a white cotton string (do not use plastic or coloured string).

Place the rolls in a double boiler or steamer and steam for about 25 minutes.

Remove from steamer, cut the thread and slice each log into concentric circles.

The health conscious can eat immediately after steaming. I deep fry the concentric steamed circles to get crispy, dark green diskettes. (This is a yummier, albeit fattening snack, but oh-so-good.)

After draining on a kitchen paper, sprinkle some chaat masala on the diskettes and serve hot.

Tongue-in-a-twist Kim

Ingredients

1 kg kim
100 g mint leaves (pudina)
150 g coriander leaves (hara dhaniya)
1 tsp cumin powder (jeera)
2 green chillies
250 g yogurt (use thick hung yogurt)
black salt to taste
1 piece wood charcoal

Method

Wash and clean coriander and mint leaves.

Blend in a mixer, with salt and yogurt and bring to a chutney consistency.

Add cumin powder.

Peel the kim and cut each into two halves.

Squeeze half the juice from each half of the kim into the chutney mix.

Cut the halves into 4 pieces each.

Mix these pieces into the chutney.

Burn the charcoal piece over a fire till well lit.

My earliest memory of kim is from winter family lunches at Nimma maasi's farmhouse. Renu and Behenji used to go to the kitchen and conjure up big bowlfuls of kim which we all used to devour. Kims are large sour citrus fruit typically available only in Himachal Pradesh and for a very short period of time in the winter. I hear that Renu's neighbour has a kim tree. So this winter, head to her house for your supply. For the uninitiated, this is a super-sour fruit chaat, incredibly addictive. Sometimes, in desperation, when kim is out of season, we use oranges but it doesn't taste as good as the real thing.

Put the charcoal in a small bowl and place on top of the kim and chutney mixture in the larger bowl.

Cover the kim bowl for 2 minutes till the charcoal smoke has seeped into the kim.

Remove the charcoal bowl.

Serve the kim immediately or it will turn bitter.

Snowdrop Cookies

Easy peasy

serves 10-12

Ingredients

¼ kg butter, softened
5 tbsp icing sugar
1¾ cups flour
1 tsp vanilla essence
1 cup chopped pecans or walnuts

Method

Beat the sugar and butter together until creamy.

To this, add flour, vanilla and nuts and mix well.

Scoop out this mix one spoon at a time, and roll into a ball.

Place the balls on a baking tray, 2" apart. (Do NOT grease the baking tray.)

Preheat the oven to 180°C.

Watch the cookies closely so they don't get burnt (they are very delicate).

When done, remove from the oven and baking tray and allow to cool.

Put icing sugar into a small bowl.

Take each cookie individually and roll gently in the icing sugar to coat it.

Arrange on a serving tray – and keep away from dogs!

These cookies, originally from New York, are a melt-in-the-mouth treat traditionally made at Christmas. They are rich in butter, look very pretty, and taste great with coffee. Often, the dogs in the household have devoured them and then suffered the wrath of Santa (aka Peggy maami, who is the baker too).

No-fuss Baked Brie

I always have a tin of Brie or Camembert in the pantry and this is my quick go-to appetizer when friends drop by. Not only is it simple, but it also makes for an elegant snack, despite its gooey, messy appearance when cut into.

Ingredients

1 can or box of Brie
1 tbsp butter
½ cup assorted nuts (I use pecans, walnuts, peanuts or whatever is at hand)
3 + 1 tbsp brown sugar
½ tsp salt
½ tsp chilli powder

Method

Place the butter in a pan.

Add the nuts, salt, chilli powder and 3 tbsp brown sugar and cook on medium heat until the sugar starts melting. As soon as it starts sticking to the nuts, remove from pan and spread out on a piece of silver foil to cool.

Preheat the oven to 180°C.

Remove Brie from the can or box and slice off the rind carefully from the top (leave the sides and bottom intact to help hold the shape).

Place in an ovenproof serving plate.

Now top the Brie (the side without rind, the circular top of the cheese, facing up) with a spoon of brown sugar and then cover with the assorted nuts.

Bake for 15-20 minutes till you see the Brie melting and losing shape.

Serve with a sliced French Baguette and some fruit (thinly sliced pears or apples or grapes).

An alternative to the candied nuts are caramelized onions which also taste pretty darn amazing. All you need to do is melt some butter in a pan and add 3 finely sliced onions and sauté over high heat. Add 2 garlic cloves (chopped) and fry on medium heat for about 15 minutes. Sprinkle 2 tsp brown sugar over the onions and cook for another 5 minutes. When browned, remove and top the Brie with this. Pop into the oven.

Teatime Banana Bread

serves 6-8

In the 1950s, Peggy maami's neighbour in Fresh Meadows, USA, used to make this bread every Christmas and send it to her. Since she moved to India, she has made it every year, and it is now firmly entrenched in the Sood household Christmas menu. Whenever you have some bananas that are extra ripe, this is the perfect way to use them.

Ingredients

½ cup + 1 tbsp butter, soft
¾ cup sugar
2 eggs
¾ cup very ripe bananas, mashed
1¼ cup flour (I use half white and
half brown)
¾ tsp baking soda
⅛ tsp salt
¼ cup walnuts, chopped (optional)

Method

Preheat the oven to 180°C
for 10 minutes.

Beat the butter until light.

Continue beating and
gradually add sugar. Keep
beating till fluffy.

Add eggs one by one, and
continue beating the mixture.

Beat in the mashed banana.

In another bowl, mix the flour, baking soda
and salt and add this mixture gradually
to the banana mixture. Keep beating until
well mixed.

Add walnuts if desired.

Line a loaf pan with 1 tbsp butter.

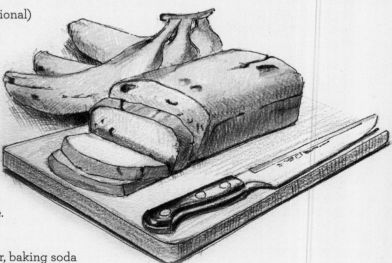

Pour the banana mix into the pan.

Bake for 40-45 minutes.

To check if ready, hit the bottom of the pan
with a spoon. If the sound is hollow, the
bread is done.

Chunky chilli cheese toast

This is my mother's Indianized version of the English snack Welsh Rarebit. It's a great hit as a chunky, solid starter for a cocktail party, though I can easily eat it for dinner too. Arjun eats it with extra chopped chillies, and insists it be made every time I visit him.

Ingredients

4 slices thick brown bread (one day old, since fresh bread will crumble easily and not hold the mix)
90 g cheddar cheese, grated; if you like strong cheese, use a sharp cheddar
2 tsp mustard powder
½ tsp chilli powder
½ tsp baking powder
2 tbsp flour
1 medium-sized egg, beaten
1 green chilli, finely chopped
1 tsp butter

Method

Preheat your oven/grill for 10 minutes at 180°C.

Mix all the ingredients, except the bread, with a wooden spatula in a bowl to form a smooth paste.

Using a spoon, place this mixture on top of the bread slices. Try not to spread it, just place it so that it forms a nice thick uneven hillocky layer.

Cover the bread completely with this mixture.

Dab a little butter on top.

Grill this in an oven until the mixture has risen to form a nice golden crust on top of the bread. (This should take around 10 minutes.)

Cut into triangles and serve with tomato sauce or Tobasco. Or even a good green chutney.

Make sure your mixture is not soggy, or the toast will become soggy too. If you like extra spice, add more chilli powder.

LA-style Pao Bhaji

Ingredients

2 potatoes, medium-sized
1 cup peas, frozen or fresh
1 cup cauliflower, broken into florets (optional)
1 cup carrot, diced
1 onion, large, chopped
3 tomatoes, chopped
2" ginger, chopped
4 garlic cloves, chopped
2 green chillies, chopped
1-2 tsp pao bhaji masala (you can substitute with a mix of 2 tsp garam masala and 1 tsp amchur powder if desperate)
1 tsp chilli powder
1 tsp cumin seeds (jeera)
1 tsp salt (or to taste)
butter (keep about 100 g at hand)
2 limes, juiced
½ cup coriander leaves, chopped
1 small onion, chopped, for the garnish
12 pao (buy from any bakery or supermarket)

When my cousin Priya was newly married and working in LA, she and her husband craved home-made Indian food, but only got time to cook on weekends. They used to host a potluck every weekend to take advantage of the culinary skills of all the Indians in the area so that everyone could indulge in good desi khaana. A Gujarati bachelor friend of theirs would always end up making this pao bhaji. They absolutely loved it and adopted the recipe. We sometimes make it at home for Sunday brunch.

Method

The bhaji:

Boil the potatoes, cauliflower, carrots and peas till soft. Add the potatoes first, after 10 minutes add the carrots, cauliflower and peas (potatoes take longer to boil).

When done, drain the water, peel the potatoes and mash all the veggies together. Don't make it a mushy mess, just mash lightly till well blended with a few semi-solid pieces so that it does not attain baby food consistency.

In a pan heat 1 tbsp butter.

When the butter is hot, add cumin seeds, chopped onions, ginger garlic and fry till the onions are translucent and the fragrance of the garlic comes wafting to your nose.

Add chopped green chillies and fry for 30 seconds.

Add tomatoes and fry for 5 minutes.

Add chilli powder and pao bhaji masala and fry till done.

Add the potato veggie mash to this mix and fry.

If the mix is too dry and you need to add water, do so a few spoons at a time.

Let the veggies simmer for about 8 minutes till fried and mixed with the spices.

Add salt.

Take off the fire and add lime juice. Mix well. Your bhaji will have a great tangy taste.

Serve in a bowl topped with chopped coriander leaves and chopped raw onions.

The pao:

Slice each pao horizontally in half.

On a flat tawa or pan, heat 2 tbsp butter.

When the butter is hot, place the pao on the melted butter until the butter gets absorbed. You can keep the pao on longer if you want it to be a bit crisp.

Serve hot.

Deelish
Home-made
Pizza

serves 4

This home-made pizza was a favourite party snack while we were growing up. Arjun used to fuss about food so much that this was offered to him as an alternative. It is better than any commercially made pizza – and all vegetarian. This recipe, however, is neither very simple nor very quick. I would recommend reading the recipe a couple of times and wrapping your head around it before you begin.

Ingredients

Pizza Base:
1 cup flour
1 sachet dry yeast (I use Tescos® dry yeast)
½ tsp sugar
3 tbsp milk
1 tsp salt
1 tsp oregano or basil (or any herb)
3 tbsp butter
1 egg
½ tsp olive oil

Sauce:
1 kg tomatoes
1 tbsp butter
1 onion, chopped
2-3 green chillies, cut long with seeds removed
1 tsp oregano
salt and pepper to taste

Toppings:
1 cup grated pizza cheese (you can use a good mozzarella)
2-3 capsicums, cleaned, deseeded and cut into roundels
1 cup button mushrooms, cleaned, sliced
8 green olives

Method

To make the base:

In a bowl, dissolve the yeast and sugar in 3 tbsp warmed milk and let it stand for a few minutes.

In a wide bowl, add the flour, salt, dried herb and mix in butter till the mixture is crumbly.

Make a small well in the middle of the flour and add the egg to it.

Add the yeast mixture to this and stir with a wooden ladle till you have a dough.

Knead the dough with your knuckles softly for about 7 minutes. Add water if too dry, but ensure it is not too wet and sticky.

Lightly grease a wide glass or plastic bowl with a spoon of oil and place the dough inside (leave ample room for the dough to expand). Make a slit a quarter way into the dough in the middle for it to proof (this is the process of the dough rising due to the yeast fermentation).

Cover with cling wrap and leave in a warm place for 2-3 hours till the dough is almost twice its original size.

Lightly punch it down again.

Make little balls from this dough and roll each ball to form 4 pizza bases that should not be more than 7 inches in diameter and just a few mm thick (think chappati thickness).

Spread some butter onto each base and bake in a preheated oven (180°C) for 15-20 minutes till cooked through. Keep cooked bases aside. (You can even store these cooked bases in the fridge for later use.)

To make the tomato sauce:

Bring a pot of water to a rolling boil. Take the tomatoes and cut an X shape on the base of each with a sharp knife to puncture the skin.

Put the tomatoes in hot water for a minute and turn off the gas. Leave the tomatoes in there for two minutes and then drain the water. Now you will find it easier to peel the skin from the X cut.

Put the tomatoes into a mixer to puree.

Fry the chopped onions and green chillies in a pan with butter.

When the onion is translucent, add the tomatoes and oregano, and fry for about 20 minutes till the sauce is nice and thick (but not dry).

Add salt and pepper to taste.

I make a huge batch of this without adding oregano and freeze and then use it for a number of things – a fish sauce for topping en-papillote (see page 76) and even as a spaghetti sauce

Assembly:

Spread tomato sauce on the pizza base.

Top with cheese, capsicum roundels and mushrooms. (At this stage you can add whatever additional toppings you prefer – pineapple chunks, aragula leaves, garlic, corn, or if you want a non-veg pizza, ham, salami or cooked mince).

Grill till the cheese is nicely browned and the capsicum is cooked.

Cut each pizza into quarters and serve.

Chatpata
Chicken Chaat

Easy peasy · serves 2

Ingredients

250 g chicken, boiled and shredded
2 tomatoes, diced
1 small capsicum, diced
1 spring onion, finely chopped
50 g coriander leaves, chopped
2 limes, juiced
1 green chilli, chopped
1 tsp black salt
1 tsp chaat masala

Method

In a bowl, mix all the ingredients together. I add the black salt and lime right at the end.

If you don't have the time to prepare chicken, you can pick up chicken tikka from the market and use it in the same way, but do away with the capsicum. You can throw in some pomegranate seeds and sliced lettuce leaves. This makes a great salad with Indian food too.

Growing up, we used to enjoy this snack when we got home from school. It's the easiest thing to make, and also a great way to use leftover boiled chicken. You can have it as a mid-morning or evening snack. It comes loaded with protein and tastes terrific.

Syrian Mutton Kabab

Easy peasy

serves 4-6

Ingredients

½ kg boneless mutton
2 tbsp vegetable oil
½" ginger, minced
½ clove garlic, minced
2 cups water
½ tsp red chilli powder
½ kg onion
20 curry leaves (kari patta)
400 g potatoes, boiled and mashed
1 green chilli, chopped
salt to taste

My cousin Priti had a colleague from Kerala, who used to bring these kababs to her office. Priti loved them and got this recipe from him. Since that day, this has been a favourite in her house. If you plan well in advance you could even freeze these and defrost and fry as an emergency snack. Priti usually serves this along with Hyderabadi daal (see page 50) and chaawal at home.

Method

In a pressure cooker, on a medium flame, add oil, ginger, garlic, mutton, water, red chilli powder and salt and give it two or three whistles.

Open the pressure cooker. Leave on fire and keep stirring, till the mutton is absolutely dry.

Take off the fire and let the mutton mixture cool.

Grind in a mixer till minced and smooth.

Slice the onion and deep fry it separately in oil with curry leaves till deep brown and crisp.

Drain the oil and keep aside.

In a pot, mix the minced mutton, mashed potatoes, green chilli and fried onions together. Check the salt at this stage because this is your last chance to put more in.

Make small round patties of the mixture.

In a non-stick pan, fry till brown on both sides. You can also make a patty, dip it in egg white and roll in breadcrumbs or panko, Japanese-style breadcrumbs, and then deep fry in oil.

Serve hot with chutney.

Quick Marie Delight

serves 4-6

Another favourite of ours while growing up, this great little snack takes 5 minutes to whip together. Once made, refrigerate and cut slices whenever hungry. It lasts for a week or two if stored in an airtight box.

Ingredients

300 g Marie biscuits
1 tin condensed milk
3 tbsp cocoa powder
¼ cup walnuts
½ cup desiccated coconut

Method

Empty the Marie biscuits into a large Ziploc® bag (or any transparent bag).

Using a rolling pin, crush the biscuits until crumbled fine.

Remove from the bag and empty into a large bowl.

Add cocoa powder and walnuts.

Using a large wooden spoon, mix in the condensed milk, stirring well.

On a flat surface lay out some cling wrap.

Pour the Marie biscuit mix onto the cling wrap and roll into a flat sheet.

Sprinkle the desiccated coconut all over.

Now carefully roll the mix from bottom to top like a Swiss roll. It will now be shaped like a log.

When done, wrap tightly in cling wrap.

Chill for at least 5 hours for it to take shape.

To serve, cut into slices.

Store in an airtight box in the fridge.

Chutneys
with Oomph

What would Indian food be without our traditional chutneys and pickles, devoid of zing and punch? In this section find some traditional pahaadi recipes that can be specifically teamed with the food and some other really yummy chutneys.

Pahaadi Chachcha

Ingredients

250 g raw mango
½ cup yogurt
4 green chillies
 cup sugar
½ tsp cumin seeds (jeera)
¾ tsp salt

Method

Peel the mangoes and slice into finger-sized pieces.

In a mixer, add mango and all the other ingredients except yogurt.

Blend for a minute.

Now add the yogurt, mix with a fork and serve.

Pahaadi Maani

serves 8-10

Ingredients

2 raw mangoes, washed well
½ l water
½ cup coriander leaves
½ cup mint leaves
2 green chillies, chopped
1 tsp cumin powder (jeera)
1 tsp salt
1 piece charcoal
1 tbsp ghee

Method

Boil water in a large pot. Add raw mangoes and cook till pulpy and tender.

Take the pot off the heat, and when the water is a little cooler, remove mangoes and peel off the skin.

Add mangoes back into the water they were boiled in. Squeeze to remove as much pulp as you can into the water. When you have only seeds, discard them.

In a mixer, add coriander leaves, mint leaves, cumin powder and salt and blend well till it forms a thick paste. Add the mango water to this and blend well.

Taste the chutney to adjust the salt.

Now you need to smoke the chutney. Heat a piece of charcoal on the fire. When well lit, place in a little bowl and pour ghee on it.

Place this bowl in the pan that contains the chutney and cover it with a lid for a few minutes to let the smoke infuse the chutney.

Remove the bowl and discard the charcoal.

Serve the maani.

Finger-licking Pahaadi Mango Stone Chutney

Somewhat easy

serves 6

Ingredients

½ kg raw mangoes
200 g jaggery (gur)
½ tsp ginger, minced
2 tsps carom seeds (ajwain)
1 tsp fennel seeds (saunf)
1 tsp red chilli powder
2 dry red chillies
1 tsp black salt or rock salt

This is an absolutely divine chutney which is called Gudumba in pahaadi. It is a sweet-and-sour raw mango chutney cooked with spices. Behenji maasi makes it best. I have embellished the original a bit since I find that adding spices works very well. Behenji maasi's version is a simpler one which uses just the jaggery and black salt and no spices. It is a little difficult and gooey to make, but worth the effort. It can be eaten with a plain parantha or rice, or even as is. You have to take the stone out and suck it clean. Yum!

Method

Wash mangoes and place in a large pan of water.

Bring to a boil and let mangoes simmer till they turn soft.

When soft, turn gas off and cool the water.

Squeeze the mangoes out of their skin while still in water and discard the skin.

Gently separate flesh from the seed, though not completely.

Boil the mango liquid with jaggery, ginger, carom seeds, fennel seeds, chilli powder and red chillies till the water becomes thick and syrupy.

Now add black salt.

Taste the mixture. If it needs more salt or chilli, now is the time to add it.

Put the seeds back in the mixture and cook for 5 minutes.

Serve hot.

Dried-in-the-sun
LIME pickle

serves many

I love lime pickle and we used to have this particular one growing up. I remember having it every time I felt nauseous on a long trip or even when I had a fever. It's great with khichdi when ill (see pages 86-87). The pickle takes between 5 to 10 days to mature. I am not crazy about the market versions which have oil in them. This is super simple to make, unlike most other pickles.

Ingredients

2 kg lime
200 g carom seeds (ajwain)
200 g rock salt, powdered

Method

Wash and cut each lime into 4 but not all the way through (it should open up like a flower but be joined at the end).

Juice 3 limes. In a large glass bowl, mix lime, salt, carom seeds and lime juice.

Empty into sealed glass jars and keep to dry in the sun for at least 5-10 days (depending on the weather). The rind will turn a nice dark brown.

Shake the jars once a day when in the sun to move the lime around and expose more surface areas to the sun.

When the rind turns soft and dark brown, the pickle is ready to eat. Check for salt. Add more if required now and shake the jar to mix.

I use Himalayan pink salt at times. If I have good-quality ginger, I slice the ginger fine and add to the mix. I also sometimes add fresh sliced raw turmeric root.

Nepali Tomato Chutney

Super easy

serves 6

Ingredients

4 tomatoes, red and ripe
8 tbsp mustard oil
1 tsp fenugreek seeds (methi)
¼ tsp red chilli powder
½ tsp ground timur (a Nepali Schezwan pepper)
1 tsp salt

Method

Heat oil in a pan.

Slice each tomato into 4.

When the oil is hot, reduce the heat and add fenugreek seeds. Wait for 10 seconds till they change colour.

Now add tomatoes, salt, timur and red chilli powder.

Cook till the tomatoes are pulpy or as they say, 'gallode'.

113

Sweet-and-sour mango chutney

Somewhat easy

serves many

Ingredients

5 kg raw mangoes
100 g red dried chillies
5 kg sugar
2 tbsp salt
500 g ginger
1 cup + 1 cup + 1 cup malt vinegar

During the mango season, our home in Bangalore was filled with raw mangoes being cut by our cook who used a traditional sickle with a wooden base which she would operate with incredible ease. It always fascinated me to see how she propped the wooden bit down with her foot and expertly sliced the mangoes. My mother would then spend two days making her famous meethi chutney, which would be sealed into jars and distributed to friends and family.

Method

Remove skin from mangoes, wash in a big bowl of salt water and slice like French fries.

Grind ginger into a coarse paste. In a large bowl add mango slices, ginger, sugar and salt. Mix well and marinate overnight (no need to refrigerate, just cover with a lid).

Soak red chillies in 1 cup malt vinegar for two hours and grind this mix together. Leave for at least an hour to infuse. (This step can be done early the next morning too.)

The next morning, take a large pot and place on the fire.

Add marinated mango mixture and let it come to a slow boil on high heat (stir constantly to avoid sugar getting too thick or sticking to the bottom).

After the first boil, add the chilli mix and bring to a simmer.

Simmer for about 45 minutes, stirring constantly.

Add 1 cup vinegar and leave on simmer. At this point, the chutney should be somewhat thick but not so sticky that you cannot get it off the back of a spoon.

If you feel the mixture is too thick, keep adding more malt vinegar ½ cup at a time.

Keep on simmer till you feel the mixture is neither too thick nor too watery and it tastes sour and sweet.

Remove from fire, let it cool and then put into sterilized jars or martabans.

114

Banana Saunth Chutney

Ingredients

75 g tamarind paste
1 tbsp vegetable oil
4 dates, soaked, deseeded and sliced
lengthwise (optional)
½ tsp cumin seeds (jeera)
2 tsp fennel seeds (saunf)
½ tsp dry onion seeds (kalonji)
¼ tsp asafoetida (hing)
1" ginger, minced
2 dry red chillies, broken
50 g jaggery (gur)
2 tbsp black salt
½ tsp chilli powder
1 cup water
2 ripe bananas, sliced

Method

In a pan, heat oil and add cumin seeds, fennel seeds, onion seeds and asafoetida.

When the seeds splutter, add ginger and red chillies and fry.

Add tamarind paste, jaggery, black salt, chilli powder and water. If using dates, add now.

Boil for 25 minutes and taste.

If you would like it to be sweeter, add more jaggery. This is your basic tamarind chutney.

Take off the fire, cool and add the cut bananas.

Serve with puja ka khana.

Mind-blowing Pahaadi Hara Namak

serves many

Ingredients

1 cup green chillies
1 cup salt
6 limes, juiced

Method

Remove the stalks from the chillies and blend the salt and chilly mixture in a mixer with the lime juice. When dry, this looks like a light-green flavoured salt. To keep it in the fridge longer, keep adding lime to it occasionally.

This is probably the easiest recipe in this book, but it will set your mouth, tongue and stomach on fire. So beware. This semi-dry chutney is great to eat with sweet radish on a sunny winter Delhi afternoon. It is also great with pakodas and suchlike.

Serve up with crudités of any kind – sweet red winter carrots, sweet radish, sweet cauliflower, etc.

I sometimes add the pulp of 2 raw mangoes to this salt. It gives a really nice zing.

Radish Khimchi

serves 2-4

Ingredients

1 medium radish, grated
¾ tsp carom seeds (ajwain)
1 lime, juiced
salt to taste

Method

Combine all the ingredients and mix well.

Let it sit for 10 minutes in the fridge to chill before serving.

This chutney is made by my eldest maami in Bombay. I messaged her grandson and fellow food lover, Aatish, who sat with her to document it. She said somewhere in the recesses of her memory is another mooli recipe, but this was the only one she could think of.

Sood Grog

The Sood family always experiments with its grog be it alcoholic or non-alcoholic. I remember as children, Aditya and I, in an attempt to recreate Baileys Irish Liqueur, mixed Scotch and condensed milk and insisted it tasted like the real thing! Over the years, the family has created some signature recipes which you can find here.

Diabolical Mulled Wine

Raja maamu makes this fabulous hot wine that goes down by the gallons during the annual Christmas open house at home, where he is always behind the scenes in the kitchen, whipping up new batches of glug. Since it's so popular, he often runs out of brandy – so he substitutes vodka, which he says does not detract from the taste of the wine. I call this drink 'chhuppa rustam' because while it looks unassuming and one can consume glasses of it, the lethal amounts of alcohol in it can get you extremely high, extremely quick. It is by far my favourite poison.

Ingredients

A bottle of red wine (use an inexpensive 750 ml wine since you will be changing the taste of the wine)
250 ml brandy (do not waste your cognac)
½-¾ cup brown sugar
10 cloves
½ nutmeg, grated
5 cinnamon sticks
2 limes, juiced
2 lemon tea bags
½ l orange juice

In the summer I substitute the red wine for white, eliminate the brandy, reduce the amount of lime and add fresh fruit like chopped grapes and apple to make a summer sangria.

Method

Put the wine, brandy and all other ingredients into a large pot and place over medium heat.

Simmer the mix on a slow fire. (Do not boil, else it will kill the flavour of the wine and evaporate most of the alcohol.) When done, strain the wine so that all the dry ingredients are removed.

Store in a flask to keep hot. This is the best way to serve the wine all evening long. Some people keep simmering a pot over the fire all evening, but that really doesn't help the flavours. It tends to get over spiced and bitter.

Serve in big red wine goblets. (If the wine is very hot, while pouring put a spoon into the wine glass, so that the heat does not crack the glass.) If you are planning to make this wine for a large party, keep all the dry ingredients wrapped together for one serving in a muslin cloth. For every bottle of wine you make, dunk one muslin sachet (potli) into the simmering wine and remove after 15 minutes. The flavour will infuse well and you do not need to strain the wine every time.

Chilli Gulabi
Guava

Ingredients

1 l pack of guava juice
3 limes, juiced
2 tsp salt (I use celery salt)
5-10 drops Sriracha (Thai chilli sauce)
4 tbsp mint leaves, roughly chopped
4 tbsp coriander leaves, roughly chopped
1 green chilli, slit lengthwise

Method

Mix all the ingredients in a large bowl. You will find that when the lime is added to the pink guava juice, it will turn a little beige.

Add the Sriracha last and go easy on it; start with 5 drops and keep tasting and adding as required.

Stir in around 15 cubes of ice since the guava juice can be rather thick, and mix well.

Taste; if you are the type who needs more chilli, salt or lime, go ahead and add more. Chill for an hour.

Pour in a Tom Collins glass and rim it with celery salt. Garnish with a green chilli.

This spiced guava drink brings back memories of my schooldays when we used to rush out after classes, to where the guava thela-walla would be sitting right outside the school bus parking lot. He would cut open for us the most delicious pink guavas and put his special mirchi masala on them. This drink is the closest I have got to that taste. It is a great drink for a Sunday brunch, especially for non-alcohol drinkers. For those who prefer spirited brunches, it can be served with a large shot of vodka.

Berliner Spiked Hot Chocolate

serves 2

Ingredients

2 strips or 100 g dark compound chocolate
(I use a brand called Morde which is
inexpensive and easily available in India)
2 cups milk
3-4 tsp sugar (you may need more
depending on how sweet you want your
hot chocolate to be)
½ tsp cinnamon powder (optional)
3 tbsp whipped cream
2 large shots rum

Method

Using a sharp knife, cut the chocolate into
little chunks.

In a pan on low heat, melt the chocolate.

Add milk and simmer. Keep stirring the
chocolate into the milk. You will see little
black chunks but stir till nicely dissolved.

Add the sugar a little at a time (keep tasting).

In a nice big cup, add a shot of rum, and top
with chocolate milk.

If you like, top it up with whipped cream.

Garnish with some cinnamon powder or
chocolate flakes.

*When I visited my friend Christiane in
Berlin, we went for a typical Sunday brunch
to the famous Prenzlauer Berg, where they
serve an all-day brunch. Despite the steady
drizzle and temperatures hovering around
4° Celsius, we sat outside the café to enjoy
the crisp air. I had this absolutely incredible
cup of hot chocolate topped with whipped
cream and spiked with rum. I replicated it at
home, and now it is a Delhi winter favourite.*

Any Season
Squash

Ingredients

1 kg fruit pulp or juice
(plums, phalsa, any
berries, lemon, even
very tart mandarin
oranges)
1½ cups sugar
1 cup water
rock salt to
taste (optional)

Method

Take the fruit and
remove pit or seeds.
For fruits like plums I
just put the deseeded fruits
in the mixer to get a juice; if it is phalsa,
which not only has a large pit but also a
tough skin, I soak in water for 30 minutes
and then squish with my hand in a large
sieve over a bowl so that I can remove the pit
and pulp at the same time.

In a pan add sugar and water. If your fruit is
very sour, you may want to add ¼-½ cup more
sugar. Heat till the sugar is dissolved and wait
till the mix is cold.

Mix the juice and sugar syrup. Pour in ¾ of the
sugar syrup first and mix and then make a trial
glass of squash to see how it tastes. (Mix 1 part
fruit and sugar mix to 3 parts water.) If you feel
it's sour, put the rest of the sugar syrup in.

*At home, after we get back from work,
there is a huge demand for nimbu
pani, Rooh Afza and the like.
I started to make these fruit-
based drinks purely because
I was tired of having nimbu
pani every day, and my sister-
in-law Nita and I enjoy them
tremendously. They are easy
to whip up and last for 10
days in the fridge without
preservatives. I try to use
tart fruit like plums, berries,
lime and mandarin oranges
simply because I prefer
that range of flavours. This
recipe is more a guideline
than an exact formula since the
flavours of your fruit will play a
large role in deciding how you
want to make this drink. Here, too, those who
prefer alcohol can add a dash of vodka with
the berry squash.*

Bottle and keep refrigerated.

I top the squash with a little bit of rock
salt. It tastes more delicious, but that's a
personal preference.

*Phalsa is great for health.
It is a wonderful antioxidant and is also
helpful in relieving urinary problems.*

Addictive Aam Panna

Easy peasy

serves 2

Ingredients

1 kg raw mango
2 l water
200 g coriander leaves
50 g mint leaves
6 green chillies
1 tsp cumin powder (jeera)
1 tsp black salt or rock salt
3 tsp regular salt
1½ cups sugar

Probably the only reason one looks forward to the Delhi summer is the incredible array of mangoes. I personally enjoy raw mango and one of the most coveted of all things mango is Behenji maasi's aam panna. This is bottled and sent to us all summer long and is probably the most delicious of all aam pannas I have had. Unlike ripe mangoes that 'heat' the body, raw aam panna actually cools since it prevents the loss of salt and iron. Also, I am told by reliable sources that it helps in subduing morning sickness.

Method

In a large pot add water, immerse the washed raw mangoes and bring to a boil.

Cook till mangoes turn soft and mushy and can be squeezed easily.

Turn the gas off and let the mangoes in the water cool.

In a mixer, add all the other ingredients and blend for 2 minutes.

When the mangoes are cool, squeeze them out of their skin using your palms.

Discard the skin and keep squeezing the rest of the mango pulp into the water until all that is left are the seeds.

Discard the seed.

Mix the rest of the ingredients into the water.

Mix well, chill and serve.

Kaapi
al-Sikandar

Ingredients

60 ml Bailey's Irish Cream
60 ml cognac/brandy (a three-star cognac will do)
1 tbsp vanilla ice cream
60 ml coffee decoction
1 tbsp crushed ice

Aditya was once an inventive cook, having spent ten years on his own in USA. But since his return his hand turns only to the occasional cocktail, although he does at times brew beer and cork wine with his father-in-law. His Kaapi al-Sikandar offers a Mangalorean take on the well-known Coffee Alexander and is inspired from the opening night of the restaurant Indian Accent.

Method

To make the coffee decoction, in an aluminium Moka pot, use a cup of water for every 2 tsp freshly ground Coorg coffee.

When the water is steaming and the coffee collects in the top chamber, take it off the heat and cool.

Dunk all the ingredients including the coffee into a blender and hit frappe or blend.

The ice should blend with the ice cream and other liquids to create a creamy frozen paste.

Pour into Martini glasses for best effect and offer at the end of a fine pre-plated meal.

Sweet Somethings

The big mantra at the Sood farm is chocolate. We eat chocolate in any and every form. The more bitter, the better. For years, Peggy maami has had three recipes that have attained legendary status in the family: Chocolate Cake, Swamp Pudding and Chocolate Pudding. If you are a stickler for really good cocoa, I would recommend this great Dutch brand called Hintz, but you can easily use Hersheys or Cadburys. Or Nilgiris if you live in Bangalore. From the dramatic to the romantic, you will find yummy recipes with flair in this section.

Swamp Pudding

serves 8-10

As a young mother, Peggy maami banked on her American recipe hand-me-downs to conjure up interesting dishes for the family. She discovered a killer pudding that her mother used to make, called Denver Chocolate Pudding. Adding her own little variation, she made it for Raja maamu and Aditya. Aditya saw its muddy, gooey consistency and said, with all the wisdom and imagination of a four-year-old, 'It looks like a swamp.' Since that day, it has been referred to as Swamp Pudding and it is by far the most revered dessert at home. If you are going to a friend's and need to carry something, I suggest you try this. It has a lingering effect on the senses, complete and utter pleasure ... ummmm.

Ingredients

¾ cup + ¼ cup sugar
1 cup flour
2 tsp baking powder
¼ tsp salt
2 tbsp butter
3 tbsp + 4 tbsp cocoa
½ cup milk
½ tsp vanilla essence
¼ cup brown sugar
1½ cups strong black coffee (cold, but not espresso)

Method

Preheat the oven to 180°C.

Sift together ¾ cup sugar, the flour, baking powder and salt. Keep aside.

In a double boiler, melt the butter and 3 tbsp cocoa.

Add to the flour mixture.

Stir the milk and vanilla essence into this mixture.

Pour into a buttered baking dish about 9" x 9".

On top of this mixture scatter the brown sugar, whatever is left of the white sugar and 4 tbsp cocoa. Do not mix this or stir it in.

Pour the coffee over. Do not stir.

Bake in a preheated oven for about 30 minutes at 180°C (if your oven is small and doesn't heat evenly or well, you may need to cook for 40 minutes).

When you take it out, the sides will be firm and would have moved inwards of the pan, but the top and centre will be sticky, mushy and maybe liquidy. Don't panic, it's actually done. (There will be chocolate sauce on the top and bottom of the dish.)

Let it stand at room temperature.

Serve the swamp pudding hot or cold, with whipped cream or ice cream.

For a homemade double boiler, use 2 bowls, one on top of the other. The lower one should be a regular pot with a wide brim, half full with water. The upper one should be a shallow wide-bottomed wok-style dish. The water from the bottom pot heats the chocolate on the top gently and prevents it from burning. Do not allow the water to boil but just simmer gently.

Every Night Chocolate Pudding

Easy peasy serves 6

Ingredients

9 tbsp cocoa
2 cups + ¼ cup milk
3 tbsp cornflour
⅓ cup sugar
¼ tsp salt
1 tsp vanilla essence

Method

Heat 2 cups milk in a double boiler till bubbles form at the edge of the milk (not boiling but almost there).

While the milk is being heated, mix the cornflour, sugar and salt in a bowl.

Stir in ¼ cup cold milk.

Add the entire mix to the hot milk in the double boiler.

Cook for 15 minutes in the boiler, stirring the pudding constantly till it thickens.

Cool slightly and add the vanilla essence.

Put in individual bowls or spoon into long-stemmed glasses for a fancier look and chill in the fridge.

Hoping to replicate Jell-O chocolate pudding, Peggy finally found this recipe and started making it in 1970 in Dehradun when Raja maamu was still teaching at the Indian Military Academy. According to the cousins, whenever any of them visited from Doon School, the first question they asked was: 'Chocolate pudding hai?' It's a bleak day when the cook doesn't make chocolate pudding and it's a night of sulking in bed. If you are not watching your waistline, you can top this with whipped cream and toasted walnuts.

You might like to try out a few variations on the theme:
Coffee Pudding: *Instead of cocoa, add 3 tsp coffee powder.* **Vanilla Pudding:** *Use only vanilla essence. No cocoa, no coffee.* **Coconut Pudding:** *Instead of the cocoa, add ½ cup desiccated coconut powder.* ***If you want to make a pie, make a base similar to the one used in the banoffee pie (see page 137) and add this to top up, chill for a few hours and serve.***

HOT LAVA chocolate BOMB

serves 8

Ingredients

375 g semi-sweet, dark chocolate (you can use Morde dark compound chocolate, which is available all over India)
50 g unsalted butter
80 g brown sugar
4 eggs, beaten
⅛ tsp salt (if you are using salted butter, don't add this)
1 tsp vanilla extract or 1 vanilla pod
50 g flour

Method

Preheat the oven to 200°C.

Take 8 ramekin moulds. Grease and dust with flour. Line the base with circular discs of baking parchment cut to the size of the ramekin base. (You can skip the parchment but this may cause the cakes to break while you tip them out.)

Melt chocolate in a double boiler and let it cool for 10 minutes.

Mix butter and sugar together.

Slowly beat in the eggs, salt and vanilla.

Add flour, and mix till well blended.

Add the chocolate and mix it to a smooth batter.

Divide batter into the lined ramekin moulds and put them in the oven for 10 minutes.

When done, slowly remove the cakes onto a small plate.

Nita says this is the dessert to make when you are short on time but need high drama on the table. These little lava bombs are solid on the outside but when you put your spoon into it, a ton of yummy hot molten chocolate streams out onto your plate.

You can do a number of things to up the drama quotient on the plate. Sprinkle the bombs with powdered sugar and take a couple of berries and place gently on top. Or you can use a wine reduction (try the one from the Poached Pears recipe on page 140) and spread it around in a ring on the plate after sliding the molten lava bomb on to it.

Infallible Chocolate Cake

Easy peasy

serves 8-10

The most sought after cake in the family (since Peggy makes it once a year now), this is a sinful dark chocolate cake. Whenever the family gets together, not only is this cake wolfed down but whatever little is left is taken home by everyone in foil wrapping. For years it has been the birthday cake for Aditya, Abhinav, Ayesha and Sonal and now me. If there is one cake recipe you should follow, it is this, it is this, it is this.

Ingredients

½ cup flour, sifted
1 tbsp baking soda
¼ tsp salt
1 cup butter (soft) +1 tbsp for each pan
2 cups finely granulated sugar
4 eggs
½ cup yogurt and ½ cup milk (mixed together)
¾ cup cocoa
⅔ cup boiling water

Method

Preheat the oven to 180°C. Rub butter and lightly dust 1 tbsp flour on three 8" cake pans or one 8" x 13" pan.

Sift the flour with baking soda and salt.

In a large bowl, mix the butter and sugar together till fluffy.

Add the eggs one at a time, beating after each addition.

Beat in the yogurt and milk combination a little at a time, alternating with 2 or 3 large spoons of the flour mixture until all has been added.

Stir the cocoa into ⅔ cup boiling water till it is dissolved.

Slowly beat this cocoa mixture into the batter and pour batter into cake pans.

Bake for 30-40 minutes or till done. (Insert a toothpick into the cake. If it comes out without any cake mix sticking to it, the cake is done.)

Oven temperatures, while standard, do vary a bit in Indian ovens. So keep checking for doneness.

For the Chocolate Icing

Ingredients

9 tbsp cocoa
4 tbsp butter
¼ tsp salt
1 tsp vanilla essence
7 tbsp milk
400 g icing sugar

Method

In a double boiler, melt the cocoa and butter. Remove from heat.

Add salt.

Add sugar a little at a time with 2 tbsp milk and beat well until all the sugar and milk have been added.

If too stiff and not soft, add a little milk. If too runny, add a bit more sugar.

Add vanilla essence.

Spread icing on sides and top of cake with a table knife after the cake is completely cooled.

Emergency ORANGE Bavarian Cream

Easy peasy

serves 8

While growing up in Bangalore, we used to entertain quite a bit, which, as kids, Arjun and I didn't really enjoy. We were paid a paltry one rupee for every room (which was below minimum wage and, in hindsight, seems like child labour) to dust the tables, fluff the cushions and carry out general clean-ups in the drawing room. Whenever there were unexpected guests, I remember Mom rushing into the kitchen to make this quick orange Bavarian cream and dunking it in the fridge. By the time cocktails and dinner were over, this dessert was ready to serve – chilled. I like it because almost everything is pre-packaged and it really is an emergency dessert. This is largely made over a double boiler, so I would recommend being armed with one before starting.

Ingredients

1 can condensed milk
2 tsp gelatin
½ cup + 1 cup orange juice
1 lime, juiced
1 cup milk
2 tbsp sugar
1 cup fresh cream
3-4 oranges, peeled and segmented
1 small sponge cake, cut lengthwise into sponge fingers

Method

Add the gelatin to ½ cup orange juice so that it softens. Keep aside.

Mix the sugar in the milk in a bowl.

Blend the sweetened milk and the remaining orange juice.

Dissolve the gelatin and orange juice mixture in a pan of hot water. Use a double boiler. Be careful not to overheat or it will solidify.

When the gelatin is dissolved, add it to the condensed milk mixture. Refrigerate for an hour or till the mixture thickens.

Whip the cream in a glass or ceramic bowl with an electric beater. Place the glass bowl over another bowl filled with ice till the cream thickens. (Beating the cream heats it up and then it could turn into butter. I use a double boiler contraption with ice at the bottom for this too.)

Take the bowl out of the fridge and fold in the cream as well as most of the fresh orange segments. Save a few for the garnish.

Soak the sponge fingers in the rest of the orange juice to make it moist but not soaked through.

Take your final serving bowl and layer it, starting with the moist sponge cake and then the condensed milk–orange mixture. You can even use individual champagne saucers to layer the mix to serve individual portions.

Refrigerate for at least an hour.

When the mixture is thick, remove from the fridge.

Garnish with fresh orange segments and serve chilled.

Goooo-ey Brownies

serves 6-8

Everyone who has a brownie recipe thinks theirs is the best. In school in Bombay, all of Insha's classmates too felt that way. Till Insha took hers to school and beat the competition by miles. Her friends then came over, ostensibly to learn how to bake them, but really to feast on the sinful indulgences. 'You make them, we will eat them' was the mantra. A great way to spend an afternoon, and they knew that they would get a doggy bag to take home. Insha is now called the Brownie Queen.

Ingredients

225 g butter
1 tsp vanilla essence
250 g castor sugar (I like to mix brown and white sugar to give it an interesting flavour)
4 eggs
100 g flour
½ tsp baking powder
75 g cocoa
½ tsp salt
100 g walnuts, toasted and chopped

On Holi, Nita makes a batch of 'bhang brownies' and they are the hit of the party. For that you just substitute 50 g of butter with bhang. And wowsa, you are truly in seventh heaven.

134

Method

In a large bowl, place the butter and ensure it reaches room temperature (becomes soft).

Add vanilla essence to butter.

Add sugar and blend with a cake whisk.

Add the eggs one at a time (ideally, break each egg into a separate bowl and then add), beating the mixture while adding until they are nicely blended.

In a separate bowl, sift the flour and add the baking powder.

Fold in the flour with the egg and sugar mixture.

Then fold in cocoa and salt until the entire mixture is thick, smooth and entirely brown. It should stick to the back of your ladle.

Add the chopped walnuts (some people prefer pecans, but they are tough to find and very expensive in India).

Lightly grease a brownie pan with some butter and spoon the mixture in. Spread the mixture evenly. You can add a few tsp of your favourite liqueur or 1 tsp instant coffee powder to give it a chocolatey coffee flavour.

Preheat your oven for 10 minutes till it has reached 180°C. Put the brownie pan in to bake for approximately 25 minutes.

Stick a toothpick inside after around 20 minutes. The brownie should have pulled away from the side of the pan but will still be soft in the middle. If the toothpick comes

Three ways to toast walnuts to enhance their nutty sweet flavour:
1. *Bake for 10 minutes, spread on a baking sheet at 180°C.*
2. *Microwave on a high heat setting for 5-6 minutes, spread on plate.*
3. *Cook on pan over high heat, stirring frequently.*

out with just a teeny-weeny bit sticking to it, your brownie is done.

Take the brownie out of the pan, and cool on a cooling wire rack. If you don't have one, turn it out of the pan into a plate.

When the mega brownie is cool, cut it into little bite-size squares.

Serve with a dollop of vanilla ice cream or even with some peanut butter spread on top.

Don't put brownies in a fridge as they dry out quick. These keep well in a tightly covered Tupperware box for a few days.

Puja Kheer

*Everyone loves a good kheer. This particular
one is made at Behenji maasi's for every puja.
So if you have friends coming over for Diwali
or some other traditional Indian festival,
this is your easy Indian dessert. What I
like about it is that it's not too sweet,
unlike the other offerings during puja.
Depending on the weather,
one can have it hot or cold.*

Ingredients

1 cup rice (soak the rice for ½ hour
and drain)
2 tsp pure ghee
2 l milk
½ cup sugar
4 cardamoms, powdered
½ coconut, grated
6 almonds, peeled and sliced thin

Method

In a heavy pan add ghee and drained rice
and fry for 2 minutes.

Add milk and sugar. Give it one boil and let
it simmer till rice gets cooked and the milk
is thick (approximately 10-15 minutes).

Add cardamom and coconut.

Transfer to serving bowl and garnish
with almonds.

Banoffee Pie

Somewhat easy · serves 2

Ingredients

1 tin condensed milk (400 g)
15 digestive biscuits (Marie biscuits will do fine)
6 tbsp butter, soft
2 bananas, chopped
¼ tbsp salt
1 cup cream (for whipping) or just use whipped cream from a can

The youngest baker in the family is my sixteen-year-old niece Oraya who started baking a year ago. She has a natural instinct and even has a FB page called Oraya's Oven. Oraya has recently started to churn out the most interesting cakes for the birthdays of her family members. But standing head and shoulders above her cakes is her banoffee pie.

Method

In a large pan that has a tight cover, place the tin of condensed milk and cover it with water. Be sure the water covers the tin. Heat for 1½ hour. If the lid is not tight enough, you can place something heavy on the tin so that it doesn't rise with the boiling water.

In the interim, crush the biscuits with butter and mix well.

In an 8" non-stick pie pan, push the butter and digestive mixture down to the base of the pan to form a crust.

Now cut the bananas into thin slices and layer the base completely with them.

Once the condensed milk is ready, open the tin carefully after cooling. The condensed milk would have turned into a beautiful caramelized toffee-coloured semi-solid mix called Dulce de Leche.

Mix the salt in and spread over the bananas to form the topmost layer.

Top with whipped cream.

I add 1 tsp grated ginger to the base to give it a zing. I also add 3 tbsp rum to the Dulce de Leche. Some even add a layer of peanut butter on the biscuit base before placing the sliced bananas on it. You can also add your own little flavours to this classic dish.

137

Comforting APPLE Crumble

Meenakshi first ate this crumble at her bua's house in Birmingham. It was the closest her bua could get to panjiri, a Punjabi sweet she missed in the UK. When Meenakshi later made it in Bombay, her in-laws loved it too — a rare occurrence since my maamiji is a great cook herself. Although her bua is no longer alive, Meenakshi and her cousins have wonderful memories to relive every time they make it.

Ingredients

6 apples, medium-sized (I like the green Granny Smiths, but some use firm red ones)
¾ cup sugar (I prefer brown sugar; if you like your crumble very sweet, add another ¼ cup)
1 tsp cinnamon, powdered
200 g flour
125 g cold butter
10 raisins (optional)

Method

Peel and core the apples. Cut into cubes. To prevent apples from turning brown when peeled, you can dunk them in cold water with lime juice in it. This also adds a slightly tart flavour to the pie.

Place cubed apples in a large pan and sprinkle sugar on top. Put it on very low heat. Stir the mix occasionally, until the apples are soft but not mushy. This is very important, else you will end up with a semi-baby-food-type pie. You need it to have a slight crunch and shape.

Add the cinnamon powder. If you don't have cinnamon powder, just toss a nice fat log of cinnamon into the stew and it will seep into the mix.

When the apples are nearly done, raise the flame to high and cook till there is no liquid left.

Meanwhile, sieve the flour in a large bowl. Add sugar and butter to prepare the crumble.

Gently mix with your fingers until it looks a bit like breadcrumbs. Make sure there are no lumps at this stage.

Line an oven-proof baking dish with butter.

Put the apple mixture at the bottom of the dish and then pour the crumble mix on top of the mixture. You can also add around 10 raisins at this stage.

Bake for approx 30 minutes at 180°C. (Remember to preheat the oven for 10 minutes.)

When the apples are bubbling nicely and the crust is crispy and golden, remove from the oven.

Serve hot with vanilla ice cream or custard.

Elegant Poached Pears

Ingredients

2 pears, peeled and cored but whole
½ bottle red wine
¼ cup brown sugar
4"-5" cinnamon
2 cloves
5 peppercorns
1 star anise
1 lime, juiced
Store-bought puff pastry dough (if you decide to go with the puff pastry shell)
50 g mascaporne
5 tsp cream
10 walnuts, grated
1 tbsp cognac (optional)

Method

Poaching the pears:

In a large pan, empty half a bottle of red wine, add all the spices and turn the heat up.

Let the wine come to a boil and then add brown sugar and lime juice.

Slide the pears in to lie down. Keep turning gently from time to time for 10-15 minutes till they turn soft and the outside of the pear takes on a beautiful wine colour.

When the pears are soft and poached, remove pan from fire and let it cool.

Remove the pears and keep aside.

For those occasions when you need drama and beauty on the dessert table, here is a lovely recipe which, while being elaborate, is a stunner.

A few months ago I went to one of my favourite Delhi restaurants, Chez Nini. After trying their Blue Cheese Pear Tart, I was inspired to try a version of my own. I did, and while it was different and pretty, it didn't quite hit the spot taste-wise. I had a coffee with Nira, the beautiful and talented chef at Chez Nini, and she gave me a few suggestions that really made the dish stand out. I've embellished and added to taste. You can make either just the poached pears with sauce or you can add a puff pastry tart shell. If you want to impress a date, this is the recipe to try.

Put the pan back on the fire and reduce the wine sauce till it's thick and sticky.

Strain the sauce of its spices.

In a separate bowl, whisk cream and mascaporne together till nice and thick.

Put this mixture into an icing bag with a star nozzle.

To assemble:

Using a pastry brush, take the wine sauce and make a pretty swirl on a plate. Warm the pears in a microwave for 30-40 seconds.

Place one poached pear standing on its base in the middle of the plate.

With the icing nozzle, pipe out the mascaporne mix into little florets near the wine sauce.

Top this with shaved walnuts and serve hot.

You can also flambé this with a little cognac.

Pears with puff pastry:

Poach the pears as described, but in white wine.

When cool, slice neatly in half.

With a sharp knife scoop out the centre with the seeds and make a cavity.

Turn the pear cavity-side down on a baking plate.

Roll out your puff pastry dough and cut out a section large enough to cover the pear.

Using a sharp knife, cover the pear and cut the dough along the edges to mould to the shape of the pear.

Make a few incisions in the dough to let the steam out when the pastry is in the oven.

Preheat the oven to 200°C for 10 minutes.

Add the pastry-covered pears.

Cook for 10-12 minutes till the pastry has 'puffed' and the outsides are brown and flaky.

Remove from the oven and turn around so that the cavity faces you. (This means the flat seed-side of the pear faces you.)

Add the mascaporne mix to the cavity.

Serve hot.

Dramatic Crêpe Suzette

Somewhat easy — serves 6

My memories of crêpe suzette are from when I was a nineteen-year-old student in Hotel Fachschule in Switzerland. We were trained in 'front-of-the-house' trolley and flambé preparation techniques and my favourite dessert was crêpe suzette. The chefs made the crêpes and all I had to do was enact the drama with flair at the table with a flambé. I loved it. I later adapted the technique and now we make it at home and serve with flambéed cognac and brandied narangis if at hand.

Ingredients

For the crêpes:

110 g flour, sifted
2 eggs (at room temperature)
200 ml milk mixed with 75 ml water
½ orange, grated, for the zest
1 tbsp caster sugar
1 tsp salt
2 tbsp + 50 g butter (at room temperature)

For the sauce:

150 ml orange juice, preferably fresh
1 orange, grated for the zest
2 limes, grated and juiced
1 tbsp caster sugar
3 tbsp Grand Marnier
50 g white butter
6 tbsp cognac

Method

For the crêpes:

Sift the flour and salt into a large mixing bowl with a sieve. Hold shoulder high while sieving so that the flour gets aerated.

Now make a well in the centre of the flour and break the eggs into it. Beat this mixture together. (I use a cake beater for this.)

Slowly add milk and water and 2 tbsp butter while beating continuously till the mixture is smooth and evenly thin.

With a ladle, stir in orange zest and caster sugar.

Melt 1 tbsp butter in a 7" non-stick pan. When the pan is hot, test pan by putting in a drop of the batter. It should start solidifying almost immediately.

Make the crêpes one at a time. Take 2 tbsp batter into the ladle and pour onto the hot pan in one go. As soon as the batter hits the hot pan, swirl it to ensure the crêpe is nicely spread all over the pan. It will take 30 seconds to cook. (You can check if the bottom is cooked and a nice golden brown by using a flat knife to lift up the bottom.)

Flip the pancake over and cook the other side for 10 seconds or so.

Slide the crêpe out of the pan and keep aside. If it looks uneven on the sides, don't worry, you can camouflage that bit in the presentation.

Again line the pan with butter and repeat the crêpe-making method till you have about 10-12 crêpes

Stack the crêpes on top of each other with butter paper in between each.

For the sauce:

Mix all the ingredients, except butter, in a bowl.

Melt the butter in a largish frying pan, pour in the sauce and allow it to heat very gently.

Now carefully put one crêpe at a time into the pan with a pair of tongs. Fold the crepe in half and then fold it again.

Your crêpe will start absorbing the lovely sauce.

The assembly:

Put the sauced crêpe carefully on a warmed plate. Add another crêpe next to it, either facing the first or side by side.

Put 2 crêpes on each plate. I add a big dollop of creamy vanilla ice cream in the centre of the plate to serve and add 2 preserved narangis too (see page 144).

To serve:

Fill a large ladle with cognac. Heat the bottom of the ladle over a flame till the alcohol catches fire. Quickly pour the flaming alcohol over the crêpes on each plate for the wow factor.

Stolen Narangi Preserve

serves many

Narangi is a small lime-sized super-sour orange. You can serve this with vanilla ice cream or crêpe suzette.

Ingredients

30 narangi
100 g sugar
200 ml water
6 cardamoms
2" cinnamon
1 vanilla pod, halved
brandy, enough to
cover the narangi

Method

In a pan, simmer sugar,
water, vanilla (cut and
scrape the vanilla off the pod
and add the scrapings plus pod), cardamom
and cinnamon until sugar has melted.

Take off the heat, cover and leave in the fridge for 2 days.

Strain the syrup through a muslin cloth to clear it of any impurities.

In a large jar, add the narangi and pour the sugar syrup till jar is half full.

Top with brandy to cover the narangi and shake well to infuse the sugar and brandy mix.

Let it marinate for 10 days.

Serve with crêpe suzette.

Index

Acknowledgements

Let me start this with a disclaimer: It is hard to think of words to acknowledge the influence of a family as large as mine, and friends as varied as mine.

First, to my maternal grandparents, who not only spawned our super-large food-crazed family in the chaos of Connaught Place, they also ensured that their pahaadi food traditions were imprinted in the DNA of their children and grandchildren!

The two most important people in my life and that of Arjun: Raja maamu and Peggy maami. They have nurtured, encouraged, protected and helped us grow into seemingly decent and capable adults. We owe them more than we can ever give back.

My mother, Rani, who always had the most delicious food on the table at all times. And showed us the value of eating Indian food with our hands, you knows what I mean. Deelish, right?

My cousin Aditya and his wife Nita, fellow foodies and fellow experimenters.

My cousin Abhinav and his wife Joanna, both of whom enhanced the American food experience in the house and are constantly helping with kitchen upgrades.

My maasis: Behenji (nobody knows her by her real name, Robindro!). 'Love is the secret ingredient in my food,' she says. Superwoman, super cook and super maasi, we run to for 'maasi ke nuske' for everything from an upset stomach to an upset heart. She has been a second mother to most of her siblings.

Nimma, the perfect hostess, who taught us to eat with a silver service at her home when we were young under her and Pani uncle's watchful eyes.

Renu, the cool, regal cook who is as kooky and lovable as they come, and her late husband Amar who served up the best pahaadi food in his kitchen.

Baby, who loves to eat, but hates to cook. Her 'half potato' story will stick even if it may not have been true! Rajnish uncle who loves to eat.

My maamus: the real women of the family, or at least in the kitchens, most of the time – who love shopping, cooking and managing their homes.

Biraji, the original food rock star who was the legend behind Khyber in Bombay, and his incredible wife, Prem Dulari or maamiji, who makes great pahaadi khaana.

Hari Om, food lover extraordinaire, who wangled out the best recipes from the best cooks in Calcutta and now reproduces them with ease, and his late wife Rama, who was the warmest of them all and the most fashionable.

Mona, whose dinner buffets are legendary in the family. We look forward to all of them. His wife Ketaki who raised the IQ of the Sood Sansar by a few hundred points.

Kaka, who most enthusiastically gave his recipe for this book and his wife, Raajika, who has incredible joie de vivre and also provided some great Sindhi recipes.

My incredibly energetic and diverse cousins

and in-laws, who are the maddest bunch of people. When we get together, the cacophony WILL drown you out.

My late cousin Babloo, who was the original Salzburg hotel management graduate, his wife Baby didi or Sarojini, who has been a great friend and her sons Amit and Rohit.

My cousin Pinky (Poonam), her husband Gopi and their daughter Nandini. Thank God, Pinky married a Mallu, we have incredible recipes from there in this book.

Tunni Bhai and Annu Didi, who are the most incredible hosts when you visit Toronto, and who still treat me like a 'little sister'. Their twin boys Abhishek and Abhimanyu. Here's to more wine cycling tours, boys.

Vipin and Meenakshi and their kids Aatish and Insha. Some of the better desserts are from their kitchens.

Yudhishthira and his wife Sunandini, their kids Krishna and Yashaswat. I was told during a family event that Yudi's arm can be twisted by a steak dinner, he loves food so much.

My late cousin Rohit, who was the most beloved of all.

My cousin Nakul, his wife Seema and my two favourite young adults, Vijay Karan and Vikram Aditya. Yes, Vikram, you are the greatest. Hope this book helps you both with the next phases of your life away from home.

Priya and her husband Shekhar, the kids Shreya, Shanaya and Rishi in Australia.

My party animal cousin Ratul, his wife Komal and their kids Armaan and Angad. All warm, all fun.

Priti and her daughters Irna and Oraya, all three of whom have been a special part of my life. Here's hoping that 'Oraya's Oven' on FB becomes more than just a part-time hobby.

Geetanjalee and her husband Deepak, incredibly warm and special, and their son Aahan. Although Geetanjalee would probably not recognize a kitchen even if she was standing in one.

Ayesha and her partner Reecha, fellow foodies and exchangers of food news and views on twitter.

Sonal and her husband Vijit, both mad, super fun, and gracious hosts with a great 'trolley' sofa.

Lohash, incredibly talented and warm and an amazing photographer.

Tara, her husband Rahul and their son Sahil.

Vikran and his wife Varghabi.

My friends with whom I have enjoyed great food from peeli-daal chaawal, to those incredible unlimited champagne brunches: My bestie Anisha Bhandary, Dhruva Talwalkar, Sashwati Banerjee, Pooja Swaika, Neena Tejpal, Christiane Rump, Geeta Misra, Simon Ferrand, Bettina Ferrand, Melanie Chapman, Guy Douglas, Mina Douglas, Harshal Shah, Catherine McMannus, Maria Joao Coutinho, Anjali and Satish, Sabita and Trishul.

Chefs and foodies who inspire with their thoughts, their food, their insights or their passion: Atul Kochhar, Manish Mehrotra, Nira Kehar, Shelly Sahay, Ritu Dalmia, Gresham Fernandes, Diya Sethi, Varun Tuli, Marryam Reshii.

Food groups on FB which have been great sources of information over the years: Arjun Sawhney's EatTreat, Atul Sikand's Sikandalous Cuisine. Foodie Tweeps I follow: @cookinacurry @rushinamg @sidmathur117 @swapanseth @finelychopped.

My patient editor Shantanu, who asked during the course of editing what Tobasco was, why I wasn't being consistent in capitalizing it if it is a brand name; what 'zest' was and kept texting me constantly to tell me how just by reading the recipes, he was getting hungry (this is his first cookbook as editor). My incredibly patient publisher, Karthika, who signed me on 5 years ago, and to whom I am just delivering. She deciphered some weird cooking processes from my head and hands and translated them on page so one could understand them.

The great marketing team at HarperCollins whom I love to pieces: Neha, who deals with the most difficult authors with her infectious smile; Iti, who always keeps learning; Ramona, who insists she is terrified of computers; Ayushi, calm and smiling; Arcopol, the one to watch; Simran, the quick learner. Also to the wonderful editorial, design, finance and production teams and of course Sukumar.

A big hug to two very successful and incredibly helpful friends from yesteryears who stepped in to quickly finish over eighty illustrations:

Ayesha Broacha, photographer extraordinaire with whom I studied almost 27 years ago in Rishi Valley. She not only did the cover illustration but many more that have helped this book look stunning. Priya Hegde, graphic and web designer, and an old classmate from Sophia High School. Her attention to detail especially with the drumstick tree is incredible. Thank you both. You made this book happen. Of course, the original artist Anusheela who kicked off this book. A big hug to the 'rock' who patiently laid out the pages, stepped in to do the back cover and layout and generally made everything look beautiful and warm: Bonita Vaz–Shimray.

My 'tribe' from Integral Coaching: the Gurus, Laura, Joanne, Anne, Kevin, Suzy, Deborah, Deb, Andrew and my friends: Carla, Sarah, Jane, Sania, Stephanie, Linda, Magda, Monika, Renee, Agathe, Kristian, Alexandros, Simone, Wendy, Tamara, Holly, Christine, Jacqui, Jed, Olivier, Gaby, Fiona and Cindy. I know I finished this book, only because I did my sitting practices (er … no) and integrated to a 5 on my good days (true this).

My partner in adventures, misadventures and semblances of love, Rajiv.

And my favourite people in the whole wide world, who also love madra-palda: Aradhana, Arianna, Adianta and Adrish – I love you infinity.

Illustration Credits

Ayesha Broacha: Front cover, Pages 2, 4, 6, 8, 9, 15, 19, 20, 23, 28, 29, 33, 45, 48, 49, 50, 51, 52, 54, 57, 58, 59, 60, 66, 68, 70, 73, 90, 92, 96, 97, 98, 100, 106, 108, 120, 121, 122, 123, 124, 128, 129, 130, 137, 142

Priya Hegde: Pages 12, 14, 17, 18, 22, 26, 27, 34, 38, 40, 42, 44, 46, 80, 84, 85, 87, 88, 89, 102, 110, 111, 112, 113, 114, 115, 116, 126, 140, 144

Anusheela: Pages 24, 30, 32, 36, 55, 56, 62, 64, 74, 75, 76, 82, 86, 94, 101, 104, 107, 118, 132, 134, 136, 138,

Ayesha Broacha: ayesha.broacha@gmail.com
www.flickr.com/photos/ayeshabroacha

Priya Hegde: priya@inika.com
www.inika.com

Anusheela: asdifferent @gmail.com